HANGED AT MANCHESTER

STEVE FIELDING

First published 2008

The History Press
The Mill, Brimscombe Port
Stroud, Gloucestershire, GL5 2QG
www.thehistorypress.co.uk

Reprinted 2009, 2010, 2012

British Library Cataloguing in Publication Data.
A catalogue record for this book is available from the British Library.

ISBN 978 0 7509 5052 7

Typesetting and origination by The History Press.
Printed in Great Britain

CONTENTS

ABOUT THE AUTHOR

S teve Fielding was born in Bolton, Lancashire, in the 1960s. He attended Bolton County Grammar School and served an apprenticeship as an engineer before embarking on a career as a professional musician. After many years recording and touring, both in Great Britain and Europe, he began writing in 1993 and had his first book published a year later. He is the author of over a dozen books on the subject of true crime, and in particular hangmen and executions.

Hanged at Manchester is the fourth in a series and follows *Hanged at Durham*, *Hanged at Pentonville* and *Hanged at Liverpool*. He compiled the first complete study of modern-day executions, *The Hangman's Record 1868–1964*, and, as well as writing a number of regional murder casebooks, is also the author of two recent titles on executioners: *Pierrepoint: A Family of Executioners* and *The Executioner's Bible: The Story of Every British Hangman of the Twentieth Century*. He is a regular contributor to magazines including the *Criminologist*, *Master Detective* and *True Crime*, and was Historical Consultant for the Discovery Channel series *The Executioners* and *Executioner: Pierrepoint* for the Crime & Investigation channel. Beside writing, he teaches maths and English at a local college.

Previous titles in the series:

Forthcoming titles in the series include:

Hanged at Leeds
Hanged at Birmingham
Hanged at Wandsworth
Hanged at Winchester

ACKNOWLEDGEMENTS

I would like to thank the following people for their help with this book. Firstly, Lisa Moore for her help in every stage in the production, but mainly with the photographs and proofreading. I offer my sincere thanks to both Matthew Spicer and Tim Leech, who have been willing to share information along with rare documents, photos and illustrations from their collections. I would also like to acknowledge the help given by Janet Buckingham, who helped to input the original data.

RESEARCH MATERIAL & SOURCES

As with my previous books on capital punishment and executions, many people have supplied information and photographs over the years, some of whom have since passed away. I remain indebted for the help with rare photographs and material given to me by the late Syd Dernley (assistant executioner), and former prison officer the late Frank McKue.

The bulk of the research for this book was done many years ago and extra information has been added to my database as and when it has become available. In most instances contemporary local and national newspapers have supplied the basic information, which has been supplemented by material found in PCOM, HO and ASSI files held at the National Record Office at Kew. I have been fortunate to have access to the Home Office Capital Case File 1901–1948, along with personal information in the author's collection from those directly involved in some of the cases.

Space doesn't permit a full bibliography of books and websites accessed while researching this project. I have tried to locate the copyright owners of all images used in this book, but unfortunately a number of them were untraceable, in the main those sourced from the National Archives (TNA:PRO). I apologise if I have inadvertently infringed any existing copyright.

A small number of the cases in this book are amended, abridged or extended versions of stories that have appeared in my previous books.

INTRODUCTION

HM Prison Manchester, formerly known as Strangeways, is one of the landmark buildings in the north of England. In its 140-year existence it has housed many infamous inmates, ranging from suffragette Christabel Pankhurt, television personality David Dickinson, former Stone Roses frontman Ian Brown, actor Jimmy Nail, and murderess Myra Hindley.

At the start of Queen Victoria's reign the city of Manchester had no gaol, and as such an agreement had been made with the Lancashire county magistrates that prisoners sentenced to terms of less than six months should be incarcerated at either Belle Vue Gaol or the New Bailey at Salford, while longer terms of imprisonment should be served at either Lancaster Prison or Liverpool's Kirkdale Gaol. With the county's population expanding due to the opportunities available following the growth of the industrial revolution, it was decided that Manchester should house its own gaol.

Situated on Southall Street, in the Cheetham area of Manchester, Strangeways was designed by Alfred Waterhouse and built to replace the archaic and soon-to-be demolished New Bailey Prison in nearby Salford. Waterhouse was aided in the design and construction of the gaol by Lt-Col Joshua Jebb, the Surveyor General of Her Majesty's Prisons, and it was Waterhouse who had successfully bid to build the adjacent Assizes Court. His winning bid was one of 940 designs tendered for the commission, and work on the courts began in 1859.

Jebb had been involved in the design of most new Victorian English prisons, but most notably the radical and modern Pentonville Prison in London, which had been completed twenty years before. The design of these new prisons was based around Jeremy Bentham's 1791 Panopticon (radial) concept, a design copied from a Russian factory which housed a central circular space where bosses could watch over workers on all shop floors from a single point. This design had first been tried in the American penal system before being adopted across Europe.

Work on the imposing red brick building began in 1861 and it was sited on land that was formally the parks and gardens of Strangeways Hall, hence the prison adopting its original name. Strangeways Gaol housed two impressive gatehouses and a large twelve-sided (or dodecagonal) hall in the centre of the cellblocks. The plan of the new prison resembled a snowflake, with six wings or cellblocks: A–F wings, which radiated from the central hall complete with a medieval-style Italian campanile bell tower. The cellblock also houses a T-shaped wing, which contain the prison administration block on the ground floor and the prison chapel above it. Another radial block contains wings G–K which again stem out from a central core. The gaol was built with a formidable chimney, standing at over 230ft, used for ventilation and heating, which towers above the high prison walls.

Work was completed in the spring of 1868 and a plaque in the entrance records the official opening date as 25 June 1868. The prison originally held 744 male and 315 female prisoners. Prisoners sentenced at the adjacent Assizes would be escorted to the gaol via a tunnel under the road that linked the two buildings together.

Following the closure of the New Bailey gaol at Salford, Strangeways took over as the execution prison for the area, and vied with Liverpool's Kirkdale Gaol as the main centre of execution for Lancashire. The first gallows was a purpose-built structure erected when required at the far end of one of the wings, close to the outer wall.

The original scaffold was erected in the grounds close to the south wing and the walls of the Assizes Court, and facing a high wall. This was standard procedure at most prisons of the day, and the condemned cell was usually in the wing closest to the scaffold. By the turn of the century the gallows had become part of one of the wings, and a description of an execution in 1913 described the gallows as thus:

COUNTY·PRISON·FOR·THE·HUNDRED·OF·SALFORD

THIS PRISON
DESIGNED·FOR·THE·CUSTODY·OF
744 MALE AND 315 FEMALE PRISONERS ON THE
"SEPARATE·SYSTEM"
OF·PRISON·DISCIPLINE·
WAS·FIRST·OCCUPIED·ON·THE·25TH·OF·JUNE·1868·HAVING·BEEN
4·YEARS·AND·6·MONTHS·IN·BUILDING·THE·COST·OF·ITS·
ERECTION·WAS·DEFRAYED·BY·A·RATE·UPON·THE·HUNDRED·
OF·SALFORD·EXCLUSIVE·OF·THE·CITY·OF·MANCHESTER·AND·
BOROUGH·OF·BOLTON·AND·BY·THE·SALE·OF·THE·SITE·AND·
MATERIALS·OF·THE·NEW·BAILEY·PRISON·IN·THE·ADJOINING·
BOROUGH·OF·SALFORD

THE·BUILDING·COMMITTEE·
JOHN·TOMLINSON·HIBBERT·ESQ·M·P·CHAIRMAN

SIR·ELKANAH·ARMITAGE·KNIGHT·
ROBERT·HEYWOOD·ESQ·
THE·REVᴰ·J·SHEPHERD·BIRLEY·CLERK·
JOHN·GRUNDY·ESQ·
ROBERT·GLADSTONE·ESQ·
SAMUEL·ASHTON·ESQ·
WILLIAM·RAYNER·WOOD·ESQ·
HENRY·LEIGH·TRAFFORD·ESQ·
NATHAN·WORTHINGTON·ESQ·
EDMUND·ASHWORTH·ESQ·
ROBERT·NEEDHAM·PHILIPS·ESQ·M·P·
JOHN·ROBINSON·KAY·ESQ·

JOHN·KAY·ESQ·
EDWARD·RILEY·LANGWORTHY·ESQ·
JOHN·PLATT·ESQ·M·P·
CHARLES·HILDITCH·RICKARDS·ESQ·
EDWARD·OWENS·ESQ·
JOHN·RICK·ESQ·
THOMAS·DICKINS·ESQ·
JOSEPH·SCHOFIELD·ESQ·
HUGH·MASON·ESQ·
JOHN·DUNCUFT·ESQ·
ARTHUR·HENRY·HEYWOOD·ESQ·
ALFRED·MILNE·ESQ·

FREDᴸ·B·C·HULTON·LAW·CLERK·
CAPTAIN·THOMAS·HENRY·MITCHELL·GOVERNOR·
ALFRED·WATERHOUSE·ARCHITECT·
HENRY·LITTLER·CLERK·OF·THE·WORKS·

Plaque to commemorate the opening of the prison in 1868. (Author's Collection)

The scaffold at Strangeways is a permanent structure in a plain brick building; glass roofed, and situated a few yards from the cell occupied by the condemned prisoners. The person going to be executed is under cover during his short walk to the gallows. After leaving his cell he crosses one corridor and walks down another at the end of which there is a door, but that does not admit entrance to the place of execution. In one of the walls of the corridor is another door unseen until it is reached. There, the condemned man turns to the left and steps immediately upon the platform of the gallows. This consists of two hinged leaves, which meet in the centre and run longitudinally along the sides of the chamber. Overhead and parallel to the meeting edges are two beams fixed close together. In the centre they are linked together with a length of stout chain at which the noose is attached. The lever pulled by the executioner is in the corner beyond the scaffold, and to the right of the door. Officials attending the execution stand upon a platform fixed at one end of the building, shut off from the drop by a brass rail. Everything is scrupulously clean, except for the handle of the lever, which apparently is never cleaned. Only a minute or two passes between the moment the hangman enters the cell to bind the prisoner with leather thongs until that when the lever is pushed and the man drops into the pit, to quiver with twitching feet after the dislocation of the neck.

By the mid-twentieth century the condemned cell and gallows room formed part of a suite of cells situated at the end of 'B' wing close to the central hall. In line with most major city prisons, Strangeways had a permanent gallows, which it retained for a number of years following the abolition of capital punishment.

Strangeways did not retain its own hangmen, but relied on engaging the official Home Office executioners when one was needed. That said, the majority of modern-day executioners hailed from the region and almost all of them would have had their first experience of life inside prison when they faced the Governor at Strangeways for a stiff vetting interview prior to being accepted for training as an executioner.

The first executioner to officiate at the gaol was William Calcraft, who had also been a regular visitor to Salford Prison. Following Calcraft's retirement in 1874, he was succeeded by William Marwood, who carried out nine executions at the prison, until shortly before his death in 1883.

Dewsbury railway worker Bartholomew Binns, who was to have a short career as an executioner, filled Marwood's position as the chief hangman of England. In a reign lasting less than a year, Binns travelled the country botching executions, staggering around the prison drunk and holding levees in nearby hotels where, for the price of a drink, he would recount his adventures.

Binns' replacement, James Berry of Bradford, made many visits to the gaol and was the executioner in charge when the first female prisoner went to the gallows. Berry wrote later that because her crimes were so despicable it was hard to feel any pity for her, but hearing her forlorn wails and cries for mercy on the night before she was to hang, the pitiful sight she made as she screamed and pleaded on the short walk to the gallows, forced him to change his mind.

Following Berry's retirement in 1891, the first of a number of local executioners were engaged at the prison. Preston-born James Billington was both a barber in Farnworth and a publican in Bolton during his career on the scaffold, and when he died in 1901, a few days after travelling to Strangeways to hang a man who had been an old friend and frequent customer at his public house, he was replaced by his middle son, William. William carried out just a handful of executions at the prison before he left the list of executioners and was sent to Wakefield Gaol himself, having been charged with deserting his wife. William's younger brother John replaced him, but his career also ended suddenly in the summer of 1905 after he suffered an accident while on duty at Leeds Prison. He died a few months later from his injuries.

Henry 'Harry' Pierrepoint had been living in Manchester and working in a Prestwich furniture shop when he had applied to become a hangman. Following an interview with Governor Cruickshank at Strangeways, he was then invited to travel down to London's Newgate Gaol for training and a short time later received the offer to assist at an execution at Strangeways. The prisoner in this case was reprieved, but later that year he returned to the prison as the assistant to James Billington, in what turned out to be Billington's last execution. Pierrepoint made several visits to Manchester in a career as a hangman that lasted until 1910, when he was sacked following a fight with one of his assistants while on duty at an execution in Chelmsford. By this time Harry had persuaded his older brother Tom to also become a hangman.

To be submitted to the High Sheriff

Memorandum of Conditions to which any Person acting as
Executioner is required to conform
––––––––––––––––––

1. An executioner is engaged and paid by the High Sheriff, and is required to conform with any instructions he may receive from or on behalf of the High Sheriff in connection with any execution for which he may be engaged.

2. A list of persons competent for the office of executioner is in the possession of High Sheriffs and Governors; it is therefore unnecessary for any person to make application for employment in connection with an execution, and such application will be regarded as objectionable conduct and may lead to the removal of the applicant's name from the list.

3. Any person engaged as an executioner will report himself at the prison at which an execution for which he has been engaged is to take place not later than 4 o'clock on the afternoon preceding the day of execution.

4. He is required to remain in the prison from the time of his arrival until the completion of the execution and until permission is given him to leave.

5. During the time he remains in the prison he will be provided with lodging and maintenance on an approved scale.

6. He should avoid attracting public attention in going to or from the prison; he should clearly understand that his conduct and general behaviour must be respectable and discreet, not only at the place and time of execution, but before and subsequently. In particular he must not reveal to any person, whether for publication or not, any information about his work as an Executioner or any information which may come his way in the course of his duty. If he does he will render himself liable to prosecution under the Official Secrets Acts 1911 and 1920.

7. His remuneration will be £10 –––– for the performance of the duty required of him, to which will be added £5 –––– if his conduct and behaviour have been satisfactory. The latter part of the fee will not be payable until a fortnight after the execution has taken place.

8. Record will be kept of his conduct and efficiency on each occasion of his being employed, and this record will be at the disposal of any High Sheriff who may have to engage an executioner.

9. The name of any person who does not give satisfaction, or whose conduct is in any way objectionable, so as to cast discredit on himself, either in connection with the duties or otherwise, will be removed from the list.

10. The apparatus approved for use at executions will be provided at the prison. No part of it may be removed from the prison, and no apparatus other than approved apparatus must be used in connection with any execution.

11. The executioner will give such information, or make such record of the occurrences as the Governor of the prison may require.

Terms and conditions: two copies would be sent to the hangman each time he was offered an engagement. One copy would be retained, the other signed and returned. (Author's Collection)

The man Harry Pierrepoint had fought with at Chelmsford was Rochdale-born John Ellis, who succeeded Pierrepoint on his dismissal and went on to carry out over 200 executions in a career lasting over twenty years, including a score of executions at Manchester.

Accrington-born William Willis succeeded Ellis as the regular executioner at Strangeways in 1924. Willis had since moved to the city many years before and resided on Bunyan Street, Ardwick. His last job at the gaol was in 1926 when, instead of the usual engagement as the chief, he was appointed as the assistant to Tom Pierrepoint of Bradford at the execution of Louie Calvert. Mrs Calvert was only the second woman to be hanged at the prison and although her crime and trial had taken place in Leeds, the Yorkshire gaol no longer housed women for execution. She would be the first of many Yorkshire killers to cross the Pennines for execution at Manchester in the twentieth century. Pierrepoint, whose domain was mainly Yorkshire and the east side of the country, was presumably engaged ahead of Willis as it was the Yorkshire authorities who were responsible for recruiting the executioner, and they had chosen their own man.

A few weeks after Mrs Calvert walked to the gallows, Willis was dismissed following an incident at Pentonville, and he was then replaced as chief executioner at the prison by Tom Pierrepoint. Pierrepoint had first worked at Strangeways as the assistant to his brother in 1909, and worked as a hangman until he was well into his seventies, becoming the longest-serving chief executioner at Manchester. One of the last executions Pierrepoint carried out in a career lasting over forty years was that of Martin Coffey in 1946.

By the mid-1930s Tom Pierrepoint was being assisted by his nephew Albert Pierrepoint, the son of Henry, who was living with his mother on Mill Street, Failsworth. Albert succeeded his uncle as the chief executioner at the gaol and was a frequent visitor until he resigned in 1956. The reason for his resignation stemmed from a proposed execution at Strangeways.

In December 1955, Pierrepoint received a commission to hang two men at Manchester on 2 January 1956. By the time he travelled from his home on the outskirts of Preston to the prison the day before the execution, in a heavy snowstorm, one of the men had already been reprieved. Once they had viewed the prisoner, Middleton child-killer Thomas Bancroft, and had rigged the gallows, the hangmen retired to their quarters, where, after supper, they learned that the execution – due in just a few hours – had been cancelled. No man in the history of modern-day executions came closer to the gallows than Thomas Bancroft.

Pierrepoint was informed his services were no longer needed and allowed to go home. The rule at the time was that a hangman was always and only 'paid by the neck'. If a prisoner was reprieved, no matter how close to the execution, the Home Office were quite rigid in applying this rule. As the weather was still very poor and travelling would have been difficult, Pierrepoint spent the night in a Manchester hotel and drove home the following day. He made a claim for expenses, for accommodation, travel and loss of income in being away from his public house for the night, but was told that they would only offer him a small sum – not enough to compensate – as a goodwill gesture. In a rage he wrote out his resignation – although it did coincide nicely with a large cheque paid for the publication of his memoirs in a Sunday newspaper!

Following Pierrepoint's resignation in 1956 and the Homicide Act of 1957, which categorised types of murder worthy of the death penalty, only two further executions took place at the prison. Both were carried out by publican Harry Allen, who at various times in the post-war years had run such hostelries as the Rawsons Arms at Farnworth, The Junction Hotel, Whitefield and The Woodman in Middleton. When the death penalty in Britain was finally rescinded, Harry Allen was never officially notified, and he technically remained on standby until his death in 1992, shortly before the last death sentence was passed on the Isle of Man.

Many local men also acted as assistant hangmen at Strangeways but without going on to become chief executioners. William Conduit of Openshaw had a brief career on the gallows in 1911; George Brown also assisted at a number of executions around the time of the First World War and had a variety of addresses in Ashton-under-Lyne, Gorton and Bolton.

Thomas Phillips of Bolton and Robert Wilson of Gorton were busy assistants in the years between the wars. Phillips was a collier in Little Lever Bolton when he became a hangman in 1922; he lived for a time in London and became a chief executioner, carrying out two executions at Wandsworth at the outbreak of the war. He was dismissed in 1940, returned to his family home in Rochdale and died in 1941. Lionel Mann also lived in Rochdale and was a regular assistant to Tom Pierrepoint before he announced his resignation in 1932: Mann's boss (at his full-time job) told him he would not be eligible for promotion as long as he worked as a hangman.

Alex Riley of Moss Side assisted at many executions during the Second World War – including that of the infamous Lord Haw Haw in London – before he offered his resignation in 1946 shortly after making his one and only visit to Strangeways. The last local men to become executioners were Robert Leslie Stewart of Chadderton, who went on to become one of the two chief executioners in the post-Homicide Act years, and Tommy Cunliffe of Hindley, near Wigan, who assisted Stewart and Harry Allen on a number of occasions in the late 1950s.

With so many local hangmen officiating it is not surprising that several of them executed friends or acquaintances: James Berry hanged his old school friend Walter Wood; publican James Billington hanged Patrick McKenna, a regular in his Bolton public house; Harry Pierrepoint executed Mark Shawcross, a neighbour he had often passed the time of day with; John Ellis hanged Ashton layabout James Hargreaves, a man he had frequently met at dog-racing handicaps. In 1950 Albert Pierrepoint executed Ashton strangler James Corbitt, a regular customer in his Hollinwood public house and someone he had often sung a duet with, although Pierrepoint admitted that they

EXECUTIONS.—TABLE OF DROPS (October, 1913).

The length of the drop may usually be calculated by dividing 1,000 foot-pounds by the weight of the culprit and his clothing in pounds, which will give the length of the drop in feet, but no drop should exceed 8 feet 6 inches. Thus a person weighing 150 pounds in his clothing will require a drop of 1,000 divided by 150 = 6⅔ feet, i.e., 6 feet 8 inches. The following table is calculated on this basis up to the weight of 200 pounds :—

TABLE OF DROPS.

Weight of the Prisoner in his Clothes.	Length of the Drop.		Weight of the Prisoner in his Clothes.	Length of the Drop.		Weight of the Prisoner in his Clothes.	Length of the Drop.	
lbs.	ft.	ins.	lbs.	ft.	ins.	lbs.	ft.	ins.
118 and under	8	6	138 and under	7	3	167 and under	6	0
119 ,,	8	5	140 ,,	7	2	169 ,,	5	11
120 ,,	8	4	141 ,,	7	1	171 ,,	5	10
121 ,,	8	3	143 ,,	7	0	174 ,,	5	9
122 ,,	8	2	145 ,,	6	11	176 ,,	5	8
124 ,,	8	1	146 ,,	6	10	179 ,,	5	7
125 ,,	8	0	148 ,,	6	9	182 ,,	5	6
126 ,,	7	11	150 ,,	6	8	185 ,,	5	5
128 ,,	7	10	152 ,,	6	7	188 ,,	5	4
129 ,,	7	9	154 ,,	6	6	190 ,,	5	3
130 ,,	7	8	156 ,,	6	5	194 ,,	5	2
132 ,,	7	7	158 ,,	6	4	197 ,,	5	1
133 ,,	7	6	160 ,,	6	3	200 ,,	5	0
135 ,,	7	5	162 ,,	6	2			
136 ,,	7	4	164 ,,	6	1			

When for any special reason, such as a diseased condition of the neck of the culprit, the Governor and Medical Officer think that there should be a departure from this table, they may inform the executioner, and advise him as to the length of the drop which should be given in that particular case.

Table of drops. An experienced executioner would often add extra inches to ensure a perfect execution. (Author's Collection)

were not close and that he didn't even know the name of his friend until he turned up at the prison to carry out the execution.

Like many prisons, Strangeways is said to have a ghost. Often sighted around the former condemned cell, on B Wing, inmates and staff have reported seeing a man wearing a dark suit and carrying a briefcase who seems to vanish into thin air when approached. Descriptions of him match those of John Ellis, the Rochdale executioner, who committed suicide in 1932.

Strangeways continued to accept both male and female prisoners until 1963, when it became exclusively male, and in 1980 it began to accept remand prisoners. The worst prison riot in Britain took place at Strangeways between 1 and 25 April 1990, and virtually destroyed some of the original buildings and many of the prison records. Almost 150 staff and fifty prisoners were injured and one prisoner was killed. Sanitation and the Victorian plumbing system was one of the key issues that had led to the trouble: slopping out, lock-up times and overcrowding were also all issues held by prisoners, but due to the prison's Grade II listed status alterations were not easy to put into place. With the riot quelled, and the month-long rooftop protest finally at an end, several of the inmates were charged with a variety of offences, with the ringleaders being charged with murder. Although the men in question were later acquitted, the riot caused over £50 million worth of damage and eventually led to the Woolfe Inquiry.

The interior of a modern execution chamber. A bag of sand filled to the weight of the prisoner is attached to the rope. The hangman would test the gallows using the sand bag, which would take out any stretch in the rope and allow him to calculate the drop accurately when resetting the traps. The folding door beyond the scaffold would be removed on the morning of the execution. Once the prisoner left the condemned cell he would be on the trapdoors in just a matter of paces. (Author's Collection)

Lancashire was home to many of the country's chief executioners in the twentieth century. Top row, from left to right: Henry Pierrepoint (Author's Collection); John Ellis (T.J. Leech Archive); William Willis (Author's Collection). Bottom row: Thomas Phillips (Author's Collection); Albert Pierrepoint (Frank McKue); Harry B. Allen (Author's Collection).

The prison was put out of tender on two occasions, in 1994 and 2001, and plans to close it down and transform old cellblocks into apartments were scrapped, mainly due to the sheer difficulty and expense of knocking through thick cell walls to make spaces the size a modern-day city dweller might appreciate.

Following the riot, the prison was rebuilt and renamed Her Majesty's Prison (HMP) Manchester. With over 1,200 inmates it continues to act as the main prison for the Manchester area. This book looks in detail at the 100 men and women who were all Hanged at Manchester.

Steve Fielding, 2008
www.stevefielding.com

1

THE BOXING DAY MURDER

Michael James Johnson, 29 March 1869

Among the revellers gathered in the Cambridge Arms Inn, Salford, there was a crowd of young men who had obviously spent the best part of that day, Boxing Day 1868, consuming large quantities of beer.

One man in particular, 19-year-old Michael Johnson, was acting so rowdily that the landlord, a Mr McDermott, found it necessary to evict him for the convenience of the other customers. Johnson at first refused to leave the vault, but when a passing policeman, Sergeant Toole, was asked to give assistance, he meekly put down his drink and went outside. Johnson and the sergeant walked down Regent Road together and the officer advised him to go home and sleep off the drink he had put away that afternoon.

As soon as the men separated, Johnson made his way back to the pub. He entered the dancing saloon and immediately created a disturbance, and when the landlord asked him to go he refused, demanding one more drink. Eventually he was persuaded to leave – but as soon as the landlord resumed his place behind the bar, Johnson re-entered through the front door and began shouting, challenging the landlord to come outside and fight.

As Johnson carried on shouting, Patrick Nurney, an itinerant musician who was earning a few shillings serving in the bar, walked over to the half-door next to Johnson. He quietly suggested to Johnson, 'Why don't you go away and not be tormenting people when you know they won't fill your drink?'

Johnson cursed at the other man and asked him what the dispute had to do with him, at the same time drawing a knife from his waistband. Nurney didn't see the blade as he ushered him to the door and, after bundling him into the street, he was just about to close the door when Johnson lunged at him. A brief struggle took place and Nurney fell to the ground with a moan as Johnson fled from the bar.

A number of the customers tended to the stricken man, lifting him onto a table where it was found that he had blood oozing from a deep wound to the thigh. He was dead by the time police arrived, and it was later found that Nurney had died as a result of the wound penetrating the femoral artery.

A search was made for the murderer, who had failed to return home. He was apprehended the next morning when police visited a house on Francis Street, Hulme, which belonged to his cousin – they found the wanted man hiding under a bed.

Johnson was convicted of wilful murder at the South Lancashire Assizes before Mr Justice Brett on 12 March 1869, and sentenced to death. The jury recommended mercy on two counts, that the crime was not premeditated, and on account of his age, but despite the request, and an appeal by the Lord Mayor of Salford, the execution was scheduled to go ahead as planned.

No one had been hanged at Manchester since the passing of the Private Executions Act in spring 1868. The previous executions had taken place outside the New Bailey prison in Salford and Johnson was to be the first to be hanged in private at the new Strangeways Gaol.

The scaffold was erected in the south wing, close to the walls of the Assize Court. There was nothing facing the drop but the high outer wall of the prison about 20ft from the scaffold. The condemned cell was at the end of the adjacent block and situated just a few feet from the scaffold.

On the fateful morning, Johnson – accompanied by the hangman, the Under Sheriff and a Roman Catholic priest – made his way to the scaffold and took his place under the beam with a firm step, repeating audibly and firmly the Litany of Jesus. After the cap was placed over his head he continued praying in a loud voice and never showed any sign of faltering. Once hangman Calcraft shook hands with him, the bolt was drawn and his body fell. He began to struggle violently, but after a few convulsive gasps life appeared extinct. The priest continued reciting the Litany for some minutes.

When the drop fell a large black flag was signalled above the prison to show that an execution had been carried out. There was a crowd outside who conducted themselves quietly and there was a complete absence of any of the brutal behaviour commonplace at public executions. When the flag was raised, a few men raised their hats in respect, and the crowd soon dispersed.

2

A DEBT OF NATURE DUE

Patrick Durr, 26 December 1870

My dear boys don't fret.
This is a debt of nature due.
I must go to the earth that gave me birth.
As so must both of you.

Last words of Patrick Durr, 26 December 1870.

The hangman had spent Christmas Day in the quarters assigned to him in the prison. Inside the condemned cell Patrick Durr spent his last Christmas counting the minutes down to the fateful hour when he would pay for his brutal crime.

Forty-two-year-old Patrick Durr had come to Manchester from Ireland and lived with his wife Catherine, also aged 42, and two sons at 1 Brighton Court, Brighton Place, in the Red Bank area of Manchester. Their home, in a part of the city popular with immigrants and the unemployed, was described as a miserable hovel, destitute of furniture and with an utter absence of any comforts. Both Durr and his wife were addicted to drink, and with little in the way of money she would often pawn anything of value to pay for more drink.

On the evening of Wednesday 17 August 1870, they had both been out drinking and had returned home late in the evening. One of their sons was away, but the youngest boy, 15-year-old Patrick, was in the house when he heard his father ask his mother where his clean shirt was. Catherine told him it was in the mangle, but Durr did not believe her. He accused her of pawning it. Durr then went downstairs and returned with a piece of rope, which he then proceeded to strangle his wife with as she lay on the bed.

'God forgive you Patsy,' she cried as he knotted the rope around her neck and pulled it tight.

Durr then walked over to his son and put his arm around his shoulder: 'She's dead now Paddy, and you'll be better off!' he told him. He then asked his son what he should do: stay at the house or go and give himself up.

Told to go to the police, Durr called on his neighbour Michael Lynch, his brother-in-law, and asked Lynch if he would accompany him to the station. Lynch told Durr that he did not want to get involved with the police and slammed the door, leaving Durr to make the journey alone.

Durr stood trial on Monday 5 December at Manchester Assizes. His defence had been insanity. It was just a short trial, with the prosecution alleging that the motive was anger at finding his wife had pawned his shirt to buy drink, and the jury took just twelve minutes to reach their verdict.

With a black cap draped on his wig Mr Justice Brett sentenced Durr to death with a warning to witnesses in the gallery that his fate should be a warning to those who belonged to the lower population who were addicted to brutal violence.

'What am I to say, my Lord?' Durr asked quietly when the verdict was passed.

On the morning of his execution Durr walked bravely to the scaffold, which was situated close to the prison wall.

'I believe my boys are out there, I want to speak to them', he said to Calcraft as the hangman stepped forward to place the cap over his head. Calcraft said he could not speak now, as it was too late.

'Oh yes I can, they are listening outside,' he said loudly. As the hangman placed the cap over his head Durr raised his voice and spoke for the last time before the hangman stepped back and reached for the lever.

Patrick Durr was hanged behind the high walls of Strangeways on Boxing Day 1870. Aware that his sons were standing outside, he tried to shout to them from the gallows. (Author's Collection)

3

A DRUNKEN KISS

Michael Kennedy, 30 December 1872

On Saturday 5 October 1872, 57-year-old Michael Kennedy purchased a pistol and ammunition, telling the shopkeeper it was to keep away thieves. Kennedy was born in Castleshaw, County Monaghan, Ireland, but had been living in Manchester for most of his life. For the past thirty-five years he had been married to his wife, Ann, and they had seven children, living happily enough at Brunswick Place, Pendleton.

Kennedy had worked as an over-looker in a local mill and had lately taken to spending most of the weekends getting drunk. This caused a lot of friction at home and there were frequent quarrels, all of which stemmed from his drinking. It also cost him his job. On Saturday afternoon, 5 October, Kennedy left his local pub, stopped off to purchase the gun, and then returned home to find his meal not ready. There was an angry exchange of words before his wife went to the kitchen to fetch his food. Kennedy then had a nap on his bed and returned downstairs a short time later and asked his wife for a kiss. As he was still clearly the worse for drink, she refused, saying she was 'not in the habit of kissing drunken folk!'

'Then though'll rue', Kennedy told her, as he reached into his jacket pocket, pulled out the pistol he had just purchased and shot her in the head.

Ann Kennedy slumped to the floor unconscious and was quickly removed to the local infirmary while her husband was taken into custody. Asked if she was dead and told she wasn't, Kennedy told the police officer that he wished she was. Three days later Mrs Kennedy died from her injuries and her husband was charged with the murder.

Kennedy pleaded insanity at the trial before Mr Justice Lush on 9 December, but the purchase of the gun earlier was claimed by the prosecution to be proof that the crime was premeditated. Kennedy's defence claimed that had taken to drink following the death of one of his children and when he later lost his job he began to drink heavily. The combination of alcohol and an old head injury had the effect that, when he drank heavily, he became mad and dangerous.

On the morning of his execution, when prisoner 4251 Michael Kennedy submitted passively to the pinioning in his cell, it was reported that he was now looking much older that his 57 years. As he took his place on the trapdoors, assistant hangman 'Smith' placed a white cap over his head, before Calcraft adjusted the noose. He then shook hands with the prisoner, stepped off the trap and pulled the lever. When it seemed to stick Calcraft shouted for Smith to 'pull it', and with a loud creak the bar slid and released the hinges. Kennedy was seen to struggle for several seconds before life became extinct.

[Note: Smith was an alias of William Marwood, who in his first year as a hangman kept his identity a secret.]

4

'THAT OLD FAGGOT OF MINE . . .'

William Flanagan, 21 December 1876

On Friday 8 September 1876, William Flanagan and Margaret Dockerty rose early and spent a day at the races, where 35-year-old Flanagan made his living as a racecourse gambler. Later that day they returned to their lodgings on Clarendon Street, Chorlton-on-Medlock, both the worse for drink.

In the early evening several of the lodgers sat around in the kitchen drinking; someone was playing the accordion, and others were singing. Margaret was in the kitchen talking to one of the lodgers when Flanagan entered and, seeing them together, he approached, slapped Margaret across the face and ordered her to her room. As he sat in the kitchen later, Flanagan complained to his landlady that Margaret, whom he had been living with as man and wife for the last eight weeks, was neglecting to feed him and treating him badly.

The following morning Flanagan entered the kitchen at 10 a.m. and told the landlady that Margaret was still drunk from the following day and wanted a couple of hours' sleep. He then walked into Kaye's Beerhouse in nearby Kennedy Street and, when asked how he was getting on, Flanagan, who appeared agitated, said, 'Badly; that old faggot of mine has robbed me yesterday of from £80 to £100.' He then ordered a bottle of ginger beer and paid for it with a half crown, telling the landlord to put the change behind the bar, adding, 'I'll leave that for my pals to have a drink with when they come in; you'll never see me anymore.'

A short time later the landlady discovered the body of Margaret Dockerty in her bed: her throat had been savagely cut down to the spinal cord, and Flanagan was picked up in Salford later that morning.

His defence, when he appeared before Mr Justice Lopes at Manchester Winter Assizes on 29 November, was that he was not of sound mind at the time he committed the murder. Flanagan was described as a drifter and a layabout, dismissed from a previous job as a sheriff's officer because he was considered insane. Evidence was shown that he had made several attempts to commit suicide – once in 1872, when he cut his own throat, and on another occasion when he threw himself out of a third floor window. This had resulted in him being committed to Withington Workhouse Lunatic Ward for six months. But despite the strong claims of insanity, the jury took less than thirty minutes to find Flanagan guilty as charged.

While on remand at Strangeways awaiting trial, Flanagan made another attempt to commit suicide when he tore a piece of metal from his drinking tin and cut his windpipe. He was taken to the medical quarters at the prison and patched up before being taken to hospital where he recovered enough to stand trial. A few days before Christmas 1876, the man who seemed to want to take his own life walked to the gallows. It was the first execution at the prison for almost four years and the first carried out at the prison as chief hangman by William Marwood.

5

THE CONSEQUENCES OF INDULGENCE

John McKenna, 27 March 1877

The man waited patiently for the boat that would take him to freedom. He had his ticket and was standing in the shadows on the Quayside at Liverpool's Clarence Dock for the night steamer that would transport him to Glasgow and away from the manhunt in his home town of Rochdale. It was Monday evening 26 February 1877 and his luck was about to run out.

As the passengers began to board the vessel he joined the queue and was about to present his ticket when two detectives stepped forward and placed him under arrest. It had taken just 48 hours to apprehend one of the most callous murderers of the day.

Irish-born John McKenna was a 25-year-old plasterer who lived with his wife at Dawson Square, off Rope Street, Rochdale. Theirs was not a happy marriage; McKenna was addicted to drink and well known in the local police courts where he had racked up a list of convictions for assault and drunkenness.

Annie McKenna was the same age as her husband and they had been married for several years, during which time she had borne him two children, and at the time of her death she had just given up her position as a maid at a nearby house due to her impending confinement. On the afternoon of 24 February, McKenna came home from work and gave his wife his week's wage, keeping some back for himself which he proceeded to spend on drink. With his money gone he returned home and demanded the rest of his wage so he could return to the pub. She refused to give him the money, but instead went out to a beerhouse with a jug and brought him back some ale.

Later that afternoon neighbours heard sounds of a struggle followed by her cries of, 'Murder! Don't kill me Jack!'

Annie McKenna fled the house and took refuge in the home of her neighbour, Mary Higgins. McKenna, who by the late evening was now quite drunk, later stormed over to the Higgins' house and demanded to see his wife. He then ordered her home – and no sooner had they set foot through the door than he launched a fearful attack on her, kicking and stamping on her as she slumped to the ground.

As Mrs McKenna lay helpless on the floor her husband was joined by Thomas O'Dea, Mary's cousin, and the two men shared a jug of ale he had brought over. Before O'Dea left the house, Annie had recovered sufficiently to hand over her purse to her cousin, who merely passed it on to McKenna.

Later that night, fearing for Mary's safety, Mrs Higgins went over to the McKenna house and, through the window, she saw McKenna throw a bucket of water over his wife before he again began kicking her. Mary shouted for another neighbour to help intervene and a fierce quarrel then ensued with McKenna and the neighbour, Henry Dunn, trading punches for several minutes.

As the fight continued outside, neighbours inside the house tended to the mortally wounded woman. At one point McKenna forced his way back into his house, pushed his way over to where his wife was being treated, lifted her head off the pillow, and punched her in the face.

Annie McKenna died from her injuries and, realising what he had done, McKenna changed his shirt and said he would go and find a policeman. Instead, he took flight and made his way to Liverpool, purchasing a ticket he hoped would lead to freedom.

At his trial before Mr Justice Manisty on 5 March the prosecution claimed it was murder committed in pure unmitigated brutal circumstances. The defence meekly suggested that McKenna had not intended to commit murder, only to beat his wife up, and therefore the charge should be one of manslaughter. It was a forlorn hope and once the judge's summing up had explained what would constitute a lessening of the charges from murder, the jury didn't even bother to leave the box before announcing they had reached their verdict. Sentencing the prisoner to death, Mr Justice Manisty said he hoped that McKenna's fate, the consequences of indulgence as he termed it, would act as a warning to others. McKenna visibly paled as sentence was passed and he was escorted from the dock.

Perhaps if there could be any justice for Annie McKenna it may be the fact that hangman Marwood, noted for his skill as an executioner, made something of a mess of the execution. When the drop fell, the prisoner on the end of the rope swung violently around in the trap and was seen to struggle, with many convulsions, as the rope swayed from side to side. It took four minutes before death could be confirmed, and as the medical report later stated, the prisoner died extremely hard.

Executioner William Marwood made a rare blunder at the execution of John McKenna. The newspapers reported he died 'extremely hard'. (Author's Collection)

6

'BECAUSE I LOVED HER . . .'

George Pigott, 4 February 1878

As the tram trundled down the hill towards Lower Broughton, Salford, on a summer afternoon in 1876, driver George Pigott was flirting with pretty 17-year-old passenger Florence Galloway, a domestic servant who was on her day off and on a visit to her mother's. By the time the passenger had alighted, he had arranged for them to meet up on the following day.

Although ten years her senior, the two began to meet up regularly and soon became lovers, but whenever Florence spoke of marriage he tried to change the subject. In the autumn of that year Pigott told Florence he was leaving Manchester and moving to Birmingham, where he had a number of friends who would help him find a new job. When Florence became distraught at the thought of them breaking up he invited her to join him and, despite her mother's reservations, she eagerly agreed to his request.

It was only when Florence discovered she was pregnant in the following year that she learned that Pigott was in fact a married man with three small children that he had abandoned, unsupported, in Ardwick. It was also around this time that Pigott began to turn violent towards her and accused her of being unfaithful to him. Florence, realising there was little chance of a happy future together, collected her possessions and, with Pigott out at work, she made her way home to Salford.

Pigott soon followed her back north, took a job as a tram driver and moved back with his wife, who forgave him for the affair with Florence. However, he still wanted his younger lover, who had by now had his child, and on 24 November her mother saw Pigott loitering near her house. She told him to go back to his wife and stay away. On 5 December he forged a letter to Florence in which he asked her to meet the sender that evening with regards to a position in a sewing shop.

Keen to find work, Florence and her mother set out that evening to see about the job, only to find Pigott waiting for them at the planned rendezvous. They got into a quarrel, whereupon he pulled out a gun and shot Florence, seriously injuring her. Pigott fled to Bolton and tried to obtain work in the mines, but he was recognised from newspaper reports and arrested for attempted murder. When Florence died from her injuries on New Year's Eve, he was then charged with wilful murder.

At his trial before Mr Justice Denman on 16 January 1878, Pigott claimed that he had not intended to shoot Florence and that he had only taken the gun to take his own life if she refused to return to him. It took the jury just twenty minutes to find him guilty of murder and Pigott fainted in the dock when sentence of death was passed on him. In the death cell he composed a final letter addressed to Florence's mother in which he stated that, 'I did not murder your daughter out of feeling of revenge, but because I loved her!'

7

DELUSIONS

James McGowan, 19 November 1878

As a result of years of heavy drinking, 55-year-old James McGowan, a Salford bleach worker, began to suffer delusions and was convinced that both his son and nephew were trying to steal from him. He was also convinced that the nephew, who he had taken a sudden and unexplained dislike to, was planning to break into his house and murder him.

McGowan told his 53-year-old wife Mary about the plans to murder him and, knowing it to be all in his head, she refused to take him seriously. On the night of 7 August 1878, McGowan and his wife were at their home on Market Street, Salford, when he thought that someone was trying to break in. Mary told him he was imagining it, and it was all caused by his drinking. They began to quarrel, and during the ensuing confrontation he threw her to the ground and kicked her. She was able to climb to her feet and they continued to struggle, during which time McGowan pulled out a pocket knife and cut her throat.

Mary slumped to the ground, dead. When McGowan realised what he had done he left the house and walked into Salford police station.

'I have to come give myself up,' he told PC Pritchard, who was manning the front desk.

'And what will that be for?' the officer asked.

'I've murdered the wife,' McGowan replied calmly.

Pritchard ordered a colleague to detain the man while he went to investigate, returning a short time later to confirm that McGowan had indeed been telling the truth. Asked where the murder weapon was, McGowan said he had dropped it down a grid on the way to the station, and when the drains were later searched it was recovered.

His confession formed the basis of the prosecution's case when he stood trial before Mr Justice Manisty at Manchester on 30 October. His defence claimed that McGowan was suffering from the DTs and at the time of the murder was insane. McGowan had made a statement following his arrest, explaining that he had killed his wife because she would not help him after he claimed that his son had stolen all the coal from his cellar and his nephew was waiting outside to kick him to death. Although a doctor who examined him claimed that McGowan seemed to be suffering from what he termed 'homicidal mania', the fact that he had been lucid when he had confessed, and had tried to dispose of the murder weapon, showed that he knew what he had done was wrong, and it was enough to send him to the gallows.

8

A CRUEL TWIST OF FATE

William Cooper, 28 May 1879

When 18-year-old William Cooper spotted Ellen Smith across the floor in a Bolton dance hall, in the summer of 1855, he hurried over to renew their acquaintance. They had grown up in the same Daubhill streets and when he asked her to dance she agreed. They spent much of that summer together and their friends and family thought them ideally suited.

Then, one evening that autumn, Cooper turned up for a meeting with Ellen only to find her talking to another man. He waited until the man walked away, then confronted her. She angrily told him not to be so jealous and when, two days later, they had another quarrel, she told him they were finished.

After just a week apart, Ellen realized she had been hasty in breaking up with Cooper and she made plans to see him again – only to learn, to her horror, that not only had he given up his job and left home, but also that he had enlisted in the East India Regiment and been posted overseas. Reluctantly and tearfully, she put him to the back of her mind, and she later met another man.

In the spring of 1859, Cooper left the army and returned to Bolton. The long years away had caused him to forget the reason for his break up with Ellen, and he was hopeful for a quick reconciliation. Unfortunately for Cooper, in a cruel twist of fate, the very day his ship landed in port, Ellen had walked down the aisle with James Mather, and when he arrived in Bolton she was away on her honeymoon. It was several months before he saw her again, by chance in a dance hall. They discussed what each had been up to since that fateful row two years earlier, and parted on pleasant terms.

In 1872 James Mather decided to seek his fortune in America and the couple split up. Mather took three of their four children with him, leaving Ellen to look after the youngest, aged 9. To make ends meet she went back to work as a barmaid at the Albert, a public house on Derby Street, leaving her daughter to be cared for by her mother.

It was by chance that Cooper, now 40 years old, married with a young family, and living and working in Kearsley, walked into the bar one evening and spotted her. When he learned she and her husband had parted he became a frequent visitor to the pub, even though it was a fair distance from his home. He soon made clear his intentions of starting up the relationship again, but any romantic feelings she had for him had long since gone, and she told him so. However, she still had a fondness for her old flame and would often flirt with him.

On St Patrick's night, 1879, the landlady of the Albert asked Ellen and another barmaid if they would like to earn some extra money by waiting on a dance she was catering for at the Bridgeman Street Assembly Hall, close to Bolton town centre. The pair agreed, and at closing time they set off down Derby Street towards the town.

When Cooper heard where she was going, he became angry. On the previous Christmas she had helped out at the hall and he had been present as a guest. He had watched her flirting with several customers and when he asked her to walk home with him she had shrugged him off and asked another man to accompany her.

Cooper asked her not to work at the hall, but she told him it was none of his business – and besides, she needed the extra money. He pleaded with her not to go, but she told him to go home and carried on walking. Cooper walked slowly behind.

They reached Trinity Street station, where he again pleaded with her not to go to the dance and when she again ignored his request he slapped her across the face. She cursed him. 'What is it with you? Why don't you just go home and mind your own wife and leave me be?'

Trinity church, Bolton. As barmaid Ellen Mather left the Albert Inn, William Cooper followed and cut her throat here. (Author's Collection)

Cooper was enraged. Grabbing her by the neck, he put his knee into her back and, forcing her head down, he withdrew a pocket knife and cut her throat.

Her friend began shrieking and within minutes a policeman arrived on the scene. Cooper calmly handed him the knife. 'You've no need to get hold of me', he told the officer, 'I'm not going to run, I've done what I intended.'

On Monday 28 April Cooper stood trial before Mr Justice Stephen at Manchester Assizes. His defence was that he was not guilty of murder, but guilty of manslaughter committed 'in a frenzy of passion'. His counsel argued that Cooper had no knowledge of what he was doing at the time of the attack, but it was in vain, and the jury took just seven minutes to find him guilty as charged.

9

DEATH BY FIRE

William Cassidy, 17 February 1880

Thirty-seven-year-old boot maker William Cassidy lived with his wife Rose Ann, 33, and their young family on Rochdale Road, Manchester. Cassidy was an industrious man and had been employed at his place of work since the age of 7. They had been married for many years, but it seems that this marriage was mostly unhappy and they rowed constantly. On one occasion in the summer of 1879, following a fierce quarrel, Cassidy picked up the poker that was nestling in the fire and burned her on the foot, leaving her screaming in agony. It was, perhaps, a foretaste of what was to follow.

On the afternoon of Sunday 9 November 1879, he and his wife had tea together at their home before he went out to the local public house where he acted as the chairman at a free and easy session. During the evening Cassidy downed several pints and boasted to a friend that he intended to kill his wife and was prepared to swing for her.

When Cassidy arrived home later that night his wife was asleep in bed. In the early hours of the following morning a policeman patrolling the road outside noticed a sudden flash and bright glow coming from the upstairs window at the Cassidy house. As he crossed the street to investigate he heard sounds of frightful screaming, and he began banging on the door until Cassidy's son opened it. Cassidy himself was sitting in the kitchen and, hurrying inside, the officer saw Mrs Cassidy stagger down the stairs naked with her skin blistered and falling from her body. Going upstairs the policeman found the bed ablaze, having been doused in paraffin.

Rose Cassidy was taken to hospital in great agony and at 2 a.m. she made a dying deposition in which she claimed to have been asleep when she woke following a flash and found the bed soaked in paraffin and alight. She heard her husband making his way down the stairs and shouted for him to help, but he ignored her cries. At 5 a.m. that morning Rose Cassidy died from her injuries and her husband was arrested for her murder.

Before Mr Justice Brett on Monday 26 January 1880 Cassidy claimed that his wife, who had been drunk at the time, must have died having fallen asleep while smoking and had accidentally knocked over the paraffin lamp.

The prosecution claimed it was a wilful and atrocious murder, which he had committed following threats to kill her. The superintendent of Manchester Fire Brigade was called to give evidence and claimed that there was no chance that the lamp had been accidentally knocked over as Cassidy had claimed, as there had been several small fires across the blanket, consistent with someone throwing the flammable liquid onto the bed and setting it alight.

Cassidy was visited on the day before his execution by his mother, accompanied by his three children, who, since his arrest, had been placed in the care of the local workhouse. He had remained confident of a reprieve until the final hours, when it was reported he went from being a strong man to showing signs of great fear of his impending fate.

10

ON HER WEDDING DAY

John Aspinall Simpson, 28 November 1881

That lovely morn I fully hoped I should become a wife
And had no fear that one so dear would take away my life
But death doth come in many forms – though painful was my lot
I pray for those I've left behind, and say, 'forget me not'.

Memorial card produced following the murder of
Annie Ratcliffe, August 1881.

John Simpson had first set his eyes on 14-year-old Annie Ratcliffe when he called into her father's public house, the Blue Bell Inn on Church Street, Preston, in the summer of 1879. Infatuated by the pretty young landlord's daughter, 19-year-old Simpson became a regular visitor. Alf Radcliffe was recently widowed and considered his daughter far too young to be courting, but the age difference aside he neither liked nor trusted Simpson, who although clearly well-educated and polite, was often out of work, living on whatever money he could scrounge or win at the racecourse. Relations between Simpson and her father soured following an altercation in the bar one afternoon. Ratcliffe accused Simpson of being lazy and a waster and barred him from the pub, warning Annie not to see him again.

The young couple wrote letters declaring their feelings for each other, with Annie increasingly fraught at her father's refusal to let them see each other, one letter declaring that she would rather die than be unable to see her lover. Annie pleaded with Simpson to speak to her father and make it clear his feelings for her were genuine. Simpson asked Ratcliffe to change his mind, telling him he had found a job in the local registry office, and that he had stopped gambling. But it was to no avail: Ratcliffe had Simpson thrown out into the street with a warning for him to stay away for good.

Her father's attitude only strengthened the bond between the young couple and they began clandestine assignations, often meeting up three times a day, whenever Simpson could slip away from the office. After secretly meeting together for almost two years, Annie found herself pregnant and, as her condition began to show, Alf Ratcliffe reluctantly signed the consent form agreeing to their request for permission to wed.

On 7 July, Ratcliffe penned his signature on the document, but told Simpson he would still not be welcome at the pub and that he had no intention of attending the wedding. Alf Ratcliffe wasn't the only one not looking forward to the wedding: caught up with the planning and with trying to win her father's blessing, Annie failed to notice her husband-to-be was not as enthralled by the impending nuptials as she was.

Monday 1 August was set as the wedding day and they arranged to meet outside the Queen's Arms. Annie was wearing her wedding dress when Simpson ushered her inside and informed her that the ceremony would have to be postponed, as the registrar wasn't available that day. Instead, it was rearranged for later in the week.

Wednesday 3 August dawned into a warm, sunny morning. This time the rendezvous was the Sir Walter Scott Inn on North Road, and at a little after 8.30 a.m. Annie arrived to find her fiancé already waiting. He smiled as they met up and as she entered the small saloon in the pub he reassured her that within the next hour they would become man and wife. They sat in the empty bar, and a few minutes later the sound of breaking glass caused the landlady's daughter to hurry into the bar, where she found Annie staggering towards her with blood pouring from a horrific throat wound. Simpson sat motionless in his chair with a bloodstained razor on the table.

Simpson was quickly arrested, and as detectives investigated the attack several things became apparent. Firstly, it had been a premeditated one; the razor used to carry out the brutal attack was identified as belonging to a Preston barber whom Simpson had visited the previous Saturday and who subsequently noticed that one of his shaving razors was missing. Secondly, and most curiously, police found that no plans had in fact been made for the wedding: no one at the registry office had any knowledge of the impending nuptials; neither was the verger at St Paul's church aware that a wedding was to take place.

Simpson's trial took place before Mr Justice Key at Manchester Assizes on 7 November. The prosecution's case was that Simpson had used Annie's infatuation with him to get her to steal money from her father's pub. When she became pregnant and her father gave his permission allowing them to wed, she decided she could no longer steal from her father. Simpson then decided that rather than marry her he would kill her.

One of his ex-girlfriends told the court that, shortly before the murder, he had told her that he had no intentions of getting married: 'to hell with marriage, I'm only after the money!'

The defence made reference to letters Annie had written to Simpson in which she declared she would rather die than not marry him. They claimed that Simpson had told Annie on the morning of her death that the wedding couldn't go ahead: heartbroken, she had taken her own life.

His counsel also claimed that Simpson's actions suggested insanity. 'Wouldn't a sane man have given her the slip and perhaps taken a boat to America?' his counsel declared.

The trial lasted one day and, summing up, Mr Justice Key dismissed the insanity plea, claiming the defence had called no medical witnesses to support this theory, nor was there any proof that she had a razor or acquired one. He added that a razor is hardly the thing a bride takes to the church on her wedding day!

11

THE LODGER

Richard Templeton, 13 February 1882

In May 1881 36-year-old Richard Templeton, a machine printer, took lodgings with Betty Scott, a divorcee with three young children, who ran a boarding house at Lowerhouse, on the outskirts of Burnley. Templeton was one of three lodgers at the house and occupied a room on the first floor, but he soon began a relationship with the landlady and she would often share his bed, as the children and her crippled brother Richard Nuttall shared her room.

For a time all was well. Templeton held a good job at the nearby printing works and they even talked about marriage. However, shortly after their engagement a chain of events that would lead Templeton to the gallows began. On 27 December, following a heavy drinking session, Templeton was dismissed from his job when he failed to turn up for work.

The following day, after a series of rows, Betty told him that she no longer wished to marry him and he was told to look for new lodgings. Templeton spent the following days in a permanent drunken state and, on the morning of 2 January 1882, he went out drinking with one of the lodgers, returning home later that afternoon drunk. He sat down to dinner with the rest of the guests, but when Betty accidentally dropped a plate next to him he accused her of treating him like a dog and stormed upstairs to his room.

Later that night Templeton crept into her bedroom, which she shared with her brother, and when she awoke she told him to get out. A few hours later he returned, tiptoed across to her bed, paused for a moment, and then slipped outside. Her brother heard a gurgling sound and, unable to leave his bed, he called his sister's name several times. The commotion woke other lodgers and when someone lit a light they found Betty Scott lying in a pool of blood, her head almost severed.

The police were called and Templeton was found in his room, pacing up and down partially naked, claiming he didn't know what he had done.

When he stood trial before Mr Justice Chitty at Manchester Assizes on 26 January, his defence was that he was unaware of his actions. The statement he made following his arrest was read to the court in which he claimed, 'I've nothing to say – my mind was so deranged at the time.' His counsel attempted to show that the prisoner was insane, but the prosecution countered this by saying there was no evidence of insanity, only of drunkenness – and this was no excuse for committing a brutal murder.

The defence then offered a weak plea of manslaughter, saying that Templeton had entered her room with the razor in an attempt to frighten her, but had slipped and accidentally cut her throat. The jury took less than thirty minutes to return a verdict of wilful murder.

12

THE BUTLER DID IT

Abraham Thomas, 12 February 1883

Captain Thomas Chester Andsell's imposing residence on Kearsley Moss on the outskirts of Bolton was known among the locals as 'The Big House'. The wealthy captain, who had long since retired from a career in the militia, employed a number of servants; numbered among these were Abraham Thomas and Mrs Christina Leigh. 24-year-old Thomas held the position of butler, while Mrs Leigh, some 15 years older, acted as housekeeper, and the complement of staff was filled with a coachman, gardener and two maids.

Presumably because of her age and maturity, Mrs Leigh was placed in charge of running the house whenever the captain was away. This wasn't the normal practice in large houses in the Victorian age, and it caused Thomas to become resentful of the authority of Mrs Leigh.

On 22 December 1882, Captain Andsell left the house to spend the holidays with his daughter in London, telling his staff he would be returning early in the New Year. The departure by the captain seemed to act as a cue for Thomas to relax his duties and begin celebrating Christmas a few days early. The following morning he was given a warning for being late on duty, and again later that afternoon he was cautioned for being drunk.

Relations between Thomas and the housekeeper became very strained for the duration of the holiday period and, when Captain Andsell returned on Wednesday 3 January 1883, Mrs Leigh informed him of the butler's unsatisfactory conduct. Thomas was informed he was being suspended from duty until the captain had chance to interview him and was told to hand his keys in.

The following morning Thomas reported for duty at the house, but reminded he was still under suspension, he was told to leave. Instead he went into the gardens, where he was seen by the gardener entering the photographic studio, which also housed the captain's hunting guns.

When Mrs Leigh came on duty she was told that Thomas was on the premises and set out at once to find him. Moments later a shot rang out from the studio. A housemaid ran to investigate and saw Thomas standing over the body of the housekeeper with a smoking gun in his hand.

Taken into custody by police Thomas offered no resistance and, when asked what had happened, he could only reply: 'I don't know. We didn't get on very well, but I didn't know what I was doing.'

Three weeks later Thomas found himself before Mr Justice Key at Manchester Assizes. There was no doubt that the figure in the dock was the man who pulled the trigger, but was he guilty of a premeditated murder, as the prosecution claimed, or insane, as the defence maintained?

His counsel claimed that Thomas suffered from a rare brain disorder, 'brain fever', and whenever he had a drink he would become insane. In the late nineteenth century doctors were still to fully understand mental illness and as a result this did little to sway the jury.

The matching pair to the gun used to commit the murder was discovered in Thomas' quarters. He had been cleaning it prior to the murder and it was fully loaded. The fact it was in his room and loaded, which was strictly against the house rules, suggested that Thomas had an ulterior motive. Had he pre-planned the shooting, and was this the gun he had intended to commit the murder with? After considering both sides of the argument the jury sided with the prosecution.

13

THE PRESTON OUTRAGE

Thomas Riley, 26 November 1883

Elizabeth Alston was separated from her husband and living alone on Back Dock Street, Preston, when she became acquainted with Thomas Riley, a 55-year-old stonemason. Riley, a widower with four grown-up children, had left his home in Bradford with his eldest son and crossed the Pennines to work on the construction of the Park Hotel at Preston.

On 27 September 1883, Riley and Mrs Alston spent the day drinking at the Bay Horse Inn, which stood a few yards from her home. As they left the bar, a neighbour saw that both seemed to be staggering down the street, with the woman clearly the worse for drink – so much so that she could barely stand without support. Later that evening another neighbour heard two voices singing at her house.

Shortly before closing time Riley returned to the Bay Horse and was in a very excited state, asking for another drink. The landlord could see he was clearly drunk and refused to serve him. He also noticed that Riley had blood on his hands, so much so that when he put his hand down on the counter he left a bloodstained handprint. Refused a drink, Riley hurried away from the pub, followed by a customer who went to Mrs Alston's house and found her lying dead in a pool of blood on the floor.

Riley, meanwhile, called at the house of friends, the Taylors, and told them he had found Liz lying on her back in a drunken stupor and that he could not wake her. Mrs Taylor, accompanied by her neighbour, went to Liz's house and found a number of other neighbours standing around the woman's body. Beside the body was a heavy shovel with a handle soaked in blood. Riley left the Taylors' house and was arrested when he came out of another nearby pub.

Taken into custody, his clothes were examined and bloodstains were found on his trousers and shirt. Charged with her murder, Riley simply replied, 'I am not guilty.'

Riley pleaded not guilty when he appeared before Mr Justice Hawkins at Manchester Assizes on 8 November. The evidence against him was mainly circumstantial, but it was enough for the jury to take a very short time to find him guilty as charged.

A petition for a reprieve received over 7,000 signatures and was presented to the Home Secretary in the hope of securing a reprieve. It was to no avail. On the morning of his execution hangman Bartholomew Binns entered the condemned cell at five minutes before the appointed hour, and as the hangman took hold of his arms and pinioned them behind his back, Riley spoke clearly, 'Don't tie me so tight, lad', as Binns wound the strap around the prisoner's elbows.

Riley walked firmly along the short passage leading from the cell to the scaffold, and as the chaplain recited the Litany, tears rolled down his face. 'This is very hard,' he said to the chaplain as they reached the drop.

He took his place on the scaffold, and although he swooned slightly as the cap and noose were placed over his head, he stood firm until the bolt was drawn and he dropped to his death.

He was given a drop of 7ft and death was reported to be instantaneous. It was Binns' fourth execution and one of the last ones that he carried out satisfactorily. He was to officiate at just a further seven and on each occasion it was reported that Binns had been drunk, unable to correctly calculate and rig the drops, and that on a number of executions the prisoners had died in great agony.

Above left: *Bartholomew Binns made just one visit to Manchester during his short reign as the country's chief executioner.* Right: *Bolton murderer Kay Howarth.* (Both Author's Collection)

14

TO START A NEW LIFE

Kay Howarth, 24 November 1884

On 3 October 1884, 37-year-old commercial traveller Richard Dugdale left his home in Wakefield and travelled into Bolton where he had a number of business appointments with town-centre publicans. After concluding business in one town-centre pub he came across an old business friend, Robert Hall, who invited Dugdale to join him for lunch and a drink.

After their meal they remained in the bar, where they were joined by 24-year-old Kay Howarth, a man well known to Hall as a local layabout and thief, and despite Hall's attempts to rid them of Howarth's presence, he was not easily put off, especially as he could see both men were likely to be carrying some money and stand him a drink or two. In fact Dugdale seemed to get on well with the younger man and bought him the first of a number of drinks.

With time pressing and business still to be done, Dugdale and the other two men headed for another public house across town where the traveller had his next appointment, and over the course of the afternoon the three men visited several other pubs. In one, Dugdale returned to the table brandishing a large cheque which he put in his bag along with the rest of the money he had collected.

By this time all three men had had a lot to drink and, at 6.15 p.m., Hall had an appointment himself at the Crown and Cushion and anxious that the now very drunk Dugdale should not be left to walk the unfamiliar streets alone with so much money, he asked Howarth to escort him back to the Wheatsheaf Hotel where he had a room booked. Howarth agreed and they were last seen heading across the town centre towards Dugdale's hotel.

Later that night a man stumbled over the body of Richard Dugdale on waste ground next to Silverwell Street. He had head and throat wounds and the horrific gash in his neck left the man in no doubt that he was dead. The police were called and found that the corpse was clutching a bloodstained knife in his hand – and there was a suicide note left beside the body. Detectives quickly reasoned that this was not a case of suicide and that the killer must have placed the knife in position and written the note in an effort to cover up the murder.

From the notebooks in Dugdale's pockets police retraced his steps and this soon led them to Robert Hall, who detectives learned had been drinking with the dead man on the previous afternoon. He was roused from his bed in the early hours, and after satisfying the police of his innocence told them he had left Dugdale in the company of Kay Howarth.

Howarth was known to detectives and when they visited his lodgings they found a number of cheques made out to Dugdale, along with his watch and chain. There were also traces of blood on Howarth's clothes.

Tried before Mr Justice Smith at Manchester Assizes in November, Howarth denied committing the murder, but the jury took just a short time to find him guilty and he was duly sentenced to death. On the eve of his execution he made a full confession and claimed he had committed the murder in order to raise the money to pay for his fare to America, where he had been once before and where he had hoped to start a new life.

15

THE MAN WHO CAME BACK

Harry Hammond Swindells, 24 November 1884

Suzannah Wild was widowed in 1877. With two young daughters to support, the youngest being just 2 years old, she was fortunate that her husband had left her well provided for. Not only was she left a thriving business dealing in German yeast, but she had also inherited almost £2,000, a terrific sum of money for the time. Her husband had also invested some of the money into an iron foundry in Oldham, and it was here in the following year that Suzannah Wild met 43-year-old Harry Swindells, who was working as a bookkeeper at the foundry.

After a short courtship the couple married and Swindells quit his post at the iron works and began to work with his wife in the yeast business. Not long into the marriage Swindells began to pester his wife for money, which he frittered away on drinking, gambling and womanising. They moved into a rented house and the newly married Mrs Swindells initially seemed to tolerate her husband's 'riotous' behaviour, as she called it, but when a friend informed her he was responsible for another woman's pregnancy, they had a massive quarrel and she threw him out of the house. She then packed her own bags and moved to another house, taking her two daughters and leaving Swindells to pay the rent.

Instead, he stole some of her money and fled to America, hoping to make a new start for himself. He settled in New York, but once he had blown the stolen money and he discovered that it wasn't the land of opportunity he had heard about he returned home to beg his wife for another chance.

Suzannah finally gave in to his pleas for reconciliation and they made another attempt at their marriage. There was, however, something else to deal with now: Suzannah's eldest daughter Mary, who was now sixteen and openly resentful to her stepfather. She was aware of the reasons for the earlier break-up of the marriage and did not welcome him back to the family with the same affection her mother did. She also realised that Swindells was really only with Suzannah for her money and her refusal to accept him began to cause problems between mother and daughter, to the extent that Mary moved out and went to stay with her late father's older brother, James Wild.

Swindells soon reverted back to his old ways and when Suzannah again caught him womanising they had another fierce quarrel, which ended when he threatened her with a revolver. She managed to wrestle the gun from him and called the police. She told him that the marriage was over, for good this time, and again she threw him out. As before he managed to take some of her money, and as in the previous year he decided to try his luck in America again, heading for Pennsylvania. This time he lasted much longer, but by the spring of 1883 his luck had run out. He decided that his best, and probably only, chance of getting hold of any money was through his wife's inheritance.

He hoped that his absence would have made her heart grow fonder but he was in for a rude awakening when he called to see her. She slammed the door in his face and told him there was no chance on earth of them getting back together. Despite this, over the next year he made repeated attempts to see her and begged for her to reconsider. They were all in vain.

On 16 July 1884, Swindells again called at the house and made a scene. This time Suzannah told her daughter Mary, who was at the house at the time, to go fetch 'Uncle Jim', who lived close by. Although 59 years old, James Wild faced up to the younger and stronger man, and told him to get out of the house. They began to fight and while Mary ran to fetch a policeman, Swindells pulled out a revolver and shot Wild in the stomach. He then fired again in the direction of his wife and as she screamed for help Swindells fled the house. Although the bullet aimed for Suzannah had missed, Wild's was to prove fatal and he died before help could be summoned.

The search for the gunman drew a blank, and after a two-week manhunt it was assumed he had fled back to America and the hunt locally was scaled down. It was something of a surprise when on 4 August police received a tip-off that Swindells had been seen on the road from Ashton to Oldham. When an officer went to investigate, they found him dressed as tramp. He initially denied he was the wanted man, but then broke down and admitted his name was Swindells.

On Thursday 6 November he appeared before Mr Justice Smith at Manchester Assizes. The only witness to the crime had been his wife, but because by law a wife could not testify against her husband she sat silently in the gallery as evidence was heard from witnesses who had seen Swindells both before the shooting and as he made his escape. It was only circumstantial evidence, but it was enough to send him to the gallows.

16

A LITTLE PROBLEM WITH MICE

Mary Ann Britland, 9 August 1886

William Waterhouse was queuing up at Hurst's Chemists on Old Street, Ashton-under-Lyne, when he was asked by chemist's assistant, William Greenhalgh, to witness a sale of three packets of Harrison's Vermin Killer. Jokingly, he declared to the customer, 38-year-old factory operator Mary Ann Britland, 'Mind you administer them scientifically, and not in too large doses, and you will get the club money!'

Replying with a straight face, Mrs Britland said, 'Oh, master, you don't suppose I could do that,' adding that she wanted the poison as she was having a little problem with mice, which were making holes in her clothes, and as Harrison's Vermin Killer contained a mixture of strychnine and arsenic she therefore had to sign the poison register.

It was just before 10 a.m. on the morning of Monday 3 May 1886, and after signing for and collecting the three packets she returned home to deal with the mice. She also looked in on her husband, who had been lying ill in the bedroom since the previous Saturday night after returning from his shift behind the bar at Heath Vaults.

Mary and Thomas Britland rented a house at 92 Turner Lane, Ashton-under-Lyne, and were friendly with her close neighbours Thomas and Mary Ann Dixon, so that when her husband showed no signs of recovery Mary Britland called round to ask Thomas Dixon to come and have a look at her husband. She sent for Dr Charles Tucker and told him that her husband had been taken ill following a drinking session the previous Saturday, and had been vomiting and stricken with a fever since that time.

A week later Thomas Britland died, and a different doctor (who had examined him shortly before his death) diagnosed epilepsy. Unbeknown to the doctor, it was the second death in the Britland household – and it therefore aroused no suspicion. Two months earlier, Mary's 19-year-old daughter Elizabeth had also died suddenly, and although the doctor who had examined her was perplexed at the sudden worsening of her condition, he reported nothing suspicious and signed a certificate that death had been due to convulsions and heart spasms.

Once her husband's death certificate had been signed, Mary, accompanied by Thomas Dixon, went into nearby Mossley to collect insurance money on her late husband from the Oddfellows Society, of which he had been a member.

Unaware of the closeness between her husband and Mrs Britland, Mary Dixon offered her a room at her house following her second bereavement. Dixon and the widow Britland may have been having an affair at this time, but it is more likely that it was she who was infatuated with him and was planning to clear a way for them to be together.

In the early hours of 14 May, Mary Dixon died in great agony, having reported feeling unwell since eating supper – prepared by Mrs Britland – the previous evening. A neighbour who helped lay out the woman's body noticed that her hands were clenched and eyes wide open and staring, similar to the death features of Mrs Britland's husband and daughter, and soon word reached the local police that something was potentially amiss.

Being the third suspicious death in as many months, detectives began to make discreet enquiries and soon discovered that a multiple murderer might well be at work in the quiet mill town streets of Ashton-under-Lyne. A post-mortem was ordered on Mary Dixon and when Mrs Britland returned

Poisoner Mary Ann Britland went to the gallows screaming in terror. She was the first of four women hanged at the prison. (Author's Collection)

home she noticed a collection of glass jars beside the body. She was horrified to find that they contained samples of the contents of the stomach and were being sent away for analysis.

The results soon came back and suggested that Mrs Dixon had been poisoned, and Mary Ann Britland was taken into custody. Detectives then ordered the bodies of Britland's husband and daughter to be exhumed – and again traces of poison were found.

Mary Ann Britland stood trial alongside Thomas Dixon on Thursday 22 July 1886 before Mr Justice Cave at Manchester Assizes. It was soon clear that Dixon was in no way guilty of the crime, or even of offering the slightest encouragement, and he was quickly acquitted.

It was found that, following the death of her daughter Elizabeth in March, Britland had claimed Elizabeth's £10 life insurance, as she had with her husband following his sudden death. Her defence was absence of motive, with her counsel contesting that the small insurance payouts were no compensation for the loss of her husband and daughter.

Following conviction she declared to the court, 'I am quite innocent, I am not guilty at all.'

She was in a state of collapse on her last morning and had to be heavily assisted to the gallows and held up on the trapdoors by two male warders while hangman Berry prepared her for execution. He later recorded that her execution was one of the most memorable of his career. Berry said that when he went to view her the night before her execution she sat on the bed moaning and rocking to and fro in abject terror.

When she realised later that night that there was to be no reprieve she began to shriek so loudly that her cries echoed around the prison walls. She continued to moan and cry throughout the night, and when Berry went to strap her arms in the morning she let out a fearful scream as he entered the cell.

'Oh God forgive me, I must have been mad!' she cried as she was led to the gallows, supported by the two male prison officers who had taken over from the female warders once the execution began. Her terror grew with each passing step until she reached the gallows – where her legs gave way and she slumped into the arms of her escort crying, 'God save me, forgive me, forgive me!'

17

NO REGRETS

Thomas Leatherbarrow, 15 February 1887

Thomas Leatherbarrow was well known to Salford police. The 47-year-old dyer, a widower with four children, had previously served a prison term for assault on his deceased wife, and since his release he had often been warned for his drunken behaviour in pubs close to his home in Pendleton.

In the months leading up to Christmas 1886, Leatherbarrow had been living with Mrs Kate Quinn, a married woman separated from her husband, for almost a year, and together they occupied an apartment in a small cottage on Franchise Street, Pendleton. Both were of intemperate habits and early in January 1887 she was forced to take time off work, having injured herself when she fell in a drunken stupor into a fire grate. As a consequence of them both being out of work, Leatherbarrow was unable to supply Mrs Quinn with money, and this resulted in a series of quarrels which culminated in murder.

On New Year's Eve 1886, they had a drunken row, and when Leatherbarrow awoke on the following morning he turned on Kate and demanded that she get up or he would 'knock her brains out'. The following day Leatherbarrow informed her he had found a job and throughout the following week he left home first thing in the morning.

On Saturday 8 January, he left the house as usual, but when he returned home, they got into a fierce row. Earlier that morning Kate Quinn, unable to work through her injury, had sent a young boy to her workplace to collect her wages and, when the boy returned, Leatherbarrow greeted him at the door and took the money from him, saying he was just about to take a drink up to Kate.

Later that afternoon Kate had another caller, and when the caller failed to get an answer she tried the door and found it locked. The woman sent her daughter to the back of the house, where she was able to gain entrance. Entering Leatherbarrow's room she found Kate Quinn lying on the bed, covered with a quilt. When the quilt was removed it was found that the unfortunate woman had been battered with a hammer, before being kicked to death with what appeared to be heavy clogs.

Leatherbarrow was apprehended in a Salford public house, where he was arrested. As he was too drunk to interrogate he was held in custody until he sobered up, at which time he made a statement to the extent that he had no regrets about what he had done and remained callous and indifferent to his fate.

He insisted on pleading guilty at his trial at Manchester Assizes and, satisfied the prisoner was aware of his action, Mr Justice Smith duly sentenced him to death.

18

A CRIME OF PASSION

Walter Wood, 30 May 1887

Walter Wood had met his pretty wife Emily Ann, known to friends and family as 'Emma', while he was working at a mill in Bury. He was 35 years old and living with his mother on Thynne Street, Bolton, and she was five years younger living with her mother on Clarendon Street, Bury. Both were recently widowed. They began courting, and when he proposed marriage, she accepted; in the winter of 1886 they took a house together on Brooklyn Street, Halliwell, Bolton.

They were happy enough until Wood suddenly lost his job as a machine fitter. From that moment the marriage rapidly deteriorated. Emma told him there was no way she was going to try to live on the 10s club money Wood was receiving while out of work. He tried desperately to find a job, but work wasn't easy to find at that time, and when he returned home after another futile search for a job she told him she was leaving.

Emma packed her bags and left Bolton, taking with her not just her daughter from the previous marriage, but also all of the family furniture, and on her return to Bury she even reverted back to her maiden name. He made several unsuccessful attempts to get her back, but she was adamant she was not prepared for a life of poverty.

'I will go and live with you again if you will get work and settle down, but not without,' she told him on a visit shortly after Christmas.

Taking her words to heart, Wood tried hard to find work and was rewarded in February 1887 when he was offered a position at Dobson and Barlow's engineering works in Bolton.

Returning to his mother's house, he was preparing to travel to see his wife in Bury when a letter arrived from her. Although the contents were never revealed, whatever she had written made him angry. He thrust the letter into his pocket and made his way to Bury. At first Emma was unwilling to speak to him, but she finally agreed and they were seen walking together on a path close to Huntley Fold Farm.

What happened next was not clear, but as they crossed a field, Wood pulled out a knife and cut her throat from ear to ear. Fatally wounded, Emma stumbled down a nearby street, with blood gushing down her floral print dress.

'My husband's cut my throat,' she said, collapsing into the arms of a passer-by. She was taken into a house, where she died from her injuries within minutes.

Despite a large police hunt, Wood went to ground. A watch was kept on all nearby sea ports, as it was believed he may have attempted to flee to America, but two days later he made an attempt to call on his mother in Bolton. Although disguised, police keeping watch on the house recognised Wood as he approached the back door and he was placed under arrest. The following day he was taken to a police station in Bury and officers had to place a cordon around him as an angry lynch mob of over 600 people tried to grab him.

Wood appeared before Mr Justice Wills at Manchester Assizes on Monday 9 May. His defence was that he had committed a crime of passion and that he was not guilty of murder but of manslaughter. The judge's summing up left the jury in no doubt as to what verdict he believed was the correct one, and they needed just six minutes to find him guilty of murder.

Walter Wood, hanged for the murder of his wife. (Author's Collection)

Hangman James Berry, an old school friend of Walter Wood. (Author's Collection)

19

ISABELLA MILLER'S REVENGE

John Alfred Gell, 15 May 1888

When 32-year-old wheelwright 'Alf' Gell moved to Manchester from his home in Horncastle, he took a room with Mrs Mary Miller at Moston. Forty-six-year-old Mary had been separated from her husband for almost a decade and ran the lodging house with her daughter, Isabella.

Gell soon began a relationship with the landlady – much to the disgust of her daughter, who told them both straight that she did not approve. Mrs Miller paid no attention to her daughter's objections and for a time there were frequent quarrels between mother and daughter.

In the winter of 1887 Gell found himself out of work. Due to his relationship with his landlady this did not cause him any immediate problems, as she did not press him for any rent, saying he could pay back anything he owed when he found work.

As spring approached Gell seemed to be making no attempt to find a job and Isabella Miller took every opportunity to chide him for being lazy and making no effort as he was 'onto a good thing' at the house. Gell responded to one of her rebukes by threatening to kill her, and when he struck her following another verbal assault, Mrs Miller decided that enough was enough. She told him that the situation could not continue as it was, and either to find either a job or fresh lodgings. Gell, it seemed, did not fancy either alternative.

Early the following morning, Thursday 1 March 1888, Gell left the house. It appeared that the threat had worked and he had gone to find work, but at noon he returned, entered quietly by the back door and attacked Mrs Miller with an axe. As she slumped to the floor mortally wounded, Gell turned on her daughter, Isabella, striking her twice on the head. Fortunately, her wounds were relatively minor and she was able to rush out into the street screaming for help.

A police officer patrolling nearby was attracted to the house by the commotion and as he approached he saw Gell fleeing down the street. He gave chase and within minutes he had managed to place him under arrest.

At his trial before Mr Justice Charles on Friday 27 April, Gell's defence was that he was not guilty of the crime, which had been committed by an unknown assailant. It was a futile plea, mainly as the main prosecution witness was the victim's daughter, who had witnessed the murderous attack. Following conviction Gell claimed he had made up his mind to murder both Mary Miller and her daughter, and then himself.

On the morning of his execution Gell told hangman Berry that he was not afraid to die, and as he reached the scaffold he asked to address the watching reporters.

'Wait a minute, I want to speak. Give me a minute Mr Berry ... it is the last request of a dying man. Do not deny me it.'

Before the drop fell, he spoke for the last time: 'Isabella Miller, I hope you have had your revenge! I die an innocent man.'

20

GAOL BREAK

John Jackson, 7 August 1888

Bradford-born John Jackson was as a plumber by day and petty thief by night. Although both 'jobs' were bringing in an income, the latter was much easier and – depending on his luck when he raided his chosen target – it was also more lucrative. In the winter of 1878, 24-year-old Jackson followed the reports on the impending trial of Charlie Peace, who was on remand at Leeds Prison charged with murder. Jackson admired the exploits of the infamous cat burglar and looked upon him as something of an idol.

On 25 February 1879, Peace was hanged and the following day, perhaps realising that his life of crime may lead him on the same path, Jackson decided to join the army. After realising that he could never accept the army way of life without indulging in petty crime, he began a number of schemes, which the army chose to ignore until, following a series of warnings, he was convicted of horse stealing in 1883. Jackson was discharged from the army and sentenced to six months imprisonment at Wakefield Gaol, but within weeks he had managed to escape and embark on a spree of crime across West Yorkshire. Eventually recaptured, he was sent to Armley Gaol, Leeds, finally being released in the summer of 1885.

He initially returned to his old stomping ground, but with his face and movements well known to the police he decided to cross the Pennines and was soon housebreaking in and around Manchester. In March 1888, when he was caught red-handed breaking into a house in Eccles, he was sentenced to six months imprisonment and taken to Strangeways.

He made himself useful at the gaol when they discovered his plumbing skills, and he became a trusted prisoner, working in the blacksmith's shop. On 19 May a gas leak was reported in the matron's house and Jackson was asked to help fix the problem. He was accompanied by a warder and managed to make a temporary repair.

Gas was soon smelt again and, on Tuesday 22 May, Jackson was called back to the matron's house, this time in the charge of warder Ralph Webb. Forty-five-year-old Webb was a popular warder and had been on good terms with the prisoner since he had started work in the blacksmith's shop.

At 4 p.m. that afternoon, the matron heard a noise in the bedroom and went to investigate. She found the door locked, and despite her calls it would not be opened. She shouted for help, and three warders arrived who were able to force the door open – whereupon they found warder Webb lying, barely conscious, in a heap on the floor. Webb was able to point to the hole in the ceiling before collapsing into a coma. He died from his injuries a short time later.

It appeared that, after completing the repair, Jackson had struck Webb on the back of the head with a hammer, fracturing his skull. He had then stolen the warder's boots and, smashing a hole in the plaster ceiling, climbed into the roof space from where, using the same hammer he had bludgeoned warder Webb with, he removed enough slates to make a gap large enough to clamber onto the roof. The matron's house backed onto Southall Street and it was a drop of just 10ft to freedom.

Jackson was at large for several weeks while a massive manhunt went on. Posters of the wanted man were plastered throughout the city, which stated that Jackson was also known as Charles Wood Firth. He was finally arrested in Bradford on 2 June, and immediately admitted he was responsible for the death of the warder. Jackson claimed he did not intend to kill him and only discovered that the blow to the head had been fatal when he read about it in the following day's newspapers.

Taken back to Manchester for trial before Mr Justice Grantham on Friday 13 July, the jury needed just six minutes to find him guilty, and a month later, like the man whose life of crime he had idolised, Jackson stepped onto the gallows platform and dropped to his death.

John Jackson. (T.J. Leech Archive)

Warder Ralph Webb, murdered during a prison gaol break. (Author's Collection)

21

HANGED ON CHRISTMAS EVE

William Dukes, 24 December 1889

For several weeks George Gordon, the area manager for a Manchester-based furniture suppliers, had forsaken his weekly visit to the Bury branch as he was expecting to do business with a customer at the firm's headquarters in Manchester. And for the last four weeks the wealthy customer, a Mr Alstead, had failed to keep the appointment, always made for a Tuesday. On the fifth no show, Gordon began to suspect it was a ploy to keep him away from the Bury shop. It was with some justification.

The Bury branch was managed by 28-year-old William Dukes, and although outwardly living happily with his wife and young family in Bolton, he was a womaniser and a client to several local prostitutes, whose favours he paid for with small items of furniture from the shop, items which he had failed to account for and which were now beginning to appear as stock shortfalls.

Tuesday was the day on which Mr Gordon usually visited the shop to check the accounts and on his last visit, at the end of August 1889, he had told Dukes there were discrepancies with the books and if it was not sorted before his next visit he would be in big trouble.

On Wednesday morning, 25 September 1889, the junior manager, 19-year-old William Tootill opened the shop, and at 9.30 a.m. George Gordon finally managed to visit the premises. Dukes, who had spotted Gordon approaching, slipped out of the back door and took sanctuary in the adjacent public house, and a short time later he arranged for a telegram to be delivered to the shop telling Tootill that if Mr Gordon called to tell him that he (Dukes) was at the Manchester branch with a client from Prestwich who had ordered a number of items to be despatched from the Bury shop that afternoon. When Dukes returned, Gordon asked to see the accounts and the two headed off to the warehouse.

At shortly after 2 p.m. a warehouseman from the Manchester branch arrived by cart to collect the Prestwich order and at the warehouse door he stumbled upon a heated argument between Dukes and Gordon. An hour later Dukes handed Tootill a note saying that Mr Gordon and the client had already set out and they needed to hurry with the delivery.

The cart set off, but despite searching for over an hour the delivery men couldn't find the address of Lime Tree House, Prestwich, and reluctantly the cart returned, fully laden, to Bury.

As Dukes unlocked the warehouse door he said that if 'Old Sam' (George's father and head of the family firm) asked where George was, to tell him he had gone to the Burnley shop. Tootill looked across at the cart driver, aware that only a couple of hours earlier Dukes had told them Gordon had accompanied the customer to Prestwich.

The following morning, anxious about the whereabouts of George Gordon, who had been missing since the previous morning, Sam Gordon and his other son Meyer called at the shop. Both knew that George was having problems with the manager, who he suspected was 'cooking the books', and they confronted him face to face.

'Where's George?' Meyer demanded.

'He's gone to the Burnley shop,' Dukes reassured them.

'Nonsense!' Meyer shouted. 'Do you know what day it was yesterday?' Dukes shook his head as Meyer continued, 'At sunset yesterday we celebrated the Jewish New Year. George would not dream of being away from his family on this day. And, anyway, the Burnley shop has closed for the holidays.'

William Dukes (left), hanged on Christmas Eve 1889 for the murder of George Gordon (right). (Both Author's Collection)

Dukes tried to offer an explanation but Meyer told him to save it for the police and, grabbing him by the arm, they escorted him out of the shop and to the local police station, where Gordon relayed his suspicions to the desk sergeant. Officers accompanied them back to search the warehouse and were immediately attracted to one of the rooms, which looked as if a fight had taken place. Furniture was knocked over and lying on a table was a bloodstained screwdriver.

Superintendent Henderson pointed to a door in the corner and asked Dukes where it led.

'It's only a cellar, there's nothing much down there,' he told him. Deciding to take a look for themselves, they descended the staircase and lit up the room with their lanterns. One policeman noticed ashes in the grate and a closer look revealed them to be the shop's accounts. In a dark corner were a number of flagstones raised and a shallow trench had begun to take shape, as if someone was preparing a grave.

'Where is my brother?' Meyer shouted at Dukes, who stood in silence next to a policeman. Across the room was a large wardrobe lying on its side. Sam Gordon asked Dukes who it belonged to and was told it was for a customer in Rochdale. Meyer went to lift it and found it very heavy.

'It's full of books', Dukes offered.

Asked for a key, Dukes said the customer had the only set, so Meyer picked up a screwdriver and forced the lock. Dukes tried to intervene, but was restrained and was forced to watch as the mystery of George Gordon's disappearance was solved.

Six weeks later Dukes stood trial before Mr Justice Charles at Manchester Assizes. He pleaded not guilty to murder and claimed Gordon had been killed accidentally during a struggle. Dukes said there had been an argument at the shop over the accounts, and Gordon had threatened to punch him. Dukes told him that he could dismiss him if he wanted to, but he had no right to hit him. He then claimed that Gordon had picked up a hammer and rushed at him, only to slip and strike his head on the fireplace. Dukes said he then panicked and hid the body in the wardrobe while he dug the shallow grave and thought up a plan to conceal what had happened.

The prosecution contested on two main points: firstly, a doctor had confirmed cause of death as by a hammer blow, and a hammer was found beside the body in the wardrobe; secondly, the elaborate plan Dukes had set to conceal the accident had been put into action long before Gordon's death, which showed that his death hadn't been an accident, but rather the working of a callous, calculated killer.

The jury agreed, and on Christmas Eve 1889, Dukes was hanged, the law decreeing that he should meet his fate on the eve of a Christian celebration, just as his victim had met his on the eve of the Jewish one.

22

'IN THE FIELD BY THE WALL'

Alfred William Turner, 19 May 1891

'Come quick – there's been a murder!' The young man called breathlessly as he hurried through the doorway of Oldham's Townfield police station. It was 8.20 p.m. on Sunday 29 March 1891, and the desk sergeant told the lad to calm down and slowly explain what had happened. He gave his name as Alfred Turner, a 20-year-old labourer at Platt's machine works, and said that an hour or so earlier he had called to see his sweetheart, 18-year-old Mary Ellen Moran. He said that they had left her lodgings and after walking down Shaw Street they passed Woodstock's Spinning Mill and entered a field where two men attacked them. Turner said he had been knocked unconscious by one of the men as the other attacked Mary with a knife.

He claimed:

> We were in the field by the wall when two men jumped over the wall and started to abuse us both. I did as long as I could with them both before I come here. Send a policeman with me; I am sure she will be dead before we get back. They will have cut her throat or something, and she will have bled to death.

At Turner's insistence PC Conway hurried back with him to the field and as they made their way from the station the officer noticed that although Turner's hands were heavily bloodstained, he did not seem to be cut or bruised, nor did he show any signs of being recently beaten unconscious. Asked how he had got blood on his hands and sleeve he claimed that he had tried to lift her stricken body off the ground, but could not manage it.

It was as they reached the spot where Turner said they would find her body that he received a nasty shock. Rather than being dead on the ground as he told the officers at the station, Mary Moran was on her feet some distance away, clutching her neck – which was oozing blood from a large throat wound.

Cut-throat killer Alfred Turner.
(T.J. Leech Archive)

'Help me!' she moaned as she saw PC Conway approach. Turner tried to hurry to her side, but was held back. The constable made Turner assist him in helping Mary to a nearby stonemason's cottage, where he asked her what had happened. She meekly pointed at Turner, but he again insisted they had been attacked by two tramps. He then made an attempt to flee the scene, but was detained by the officer and held under arrest while Mary was taken to the local hospital.

Following surgery she was able to make a statement to the effect that she had gone with Turner to the field where he had accused her of planning to leave him for another man. She denied this was true, but Turner was convinced she was about to leave him and pulled out a large black-handled knife from his pocket and cut her throat, before fleeing as she slumped to the ground. The wound had almost severed her windpipe and Mary Moran died from shock and loss of blood later that night.

One month later Turner appeared before Mr Justice Wright at Manchester charged with her murder. Turner never denied the crime, but his defence claimed he was suffering from a form of insanity called 'petit mal' and was not of sound mind when he committed the murder. The jury took just a short time to find that he was not insane, but added a recommendation for mercy to their guilty verdict.

'Give my love to my mother, Lord have mercy on me,' he sobbed, trembling violently as Berry placed the noose around his neck.

23

AFTER THE WAKES

Joseph Mellor, 20 December 1892

Joseph Mellor looked up from his workbench at the commotion that was taking place on the factory floor. Whatever had caused the interruption to the working day at Mellrose Mill, Oldham, was now approaching the storeroom where he was working, and he had a shrewd idea of what it was.

'I suppose you know what I have come for?' PC Aubrook said, addressing the 33-year-old mill worker as he reached the storeroom counter.

'Aye, it's alright,' Mellor said and went to collect his overcoat. As they made their way outside Miller passed the wages clerk and spoke to him: 'Pay me up, Robert. I shan't be coming back,' he said ruefully as he left the premises.

It had been a neighbour's suspicions that had sent the policeman to the mill. On Saturday afternoon 3 September 1892, 36-year-old Mary Jane 'Jenny' Mellor had been out for a walk with the daughter of her neighbour Emma Chadwick. When she returned the child to its mother, Jenny told Emma she was thinking of going to see her own mother in Hyde later 'if the weather holds up.' It was the last time she was seen alive.

The following Monday the mills and factories of Oldham went back to work following the traditional late summer 'wakes' holiday, and for the next fortnight the regular 'knocker upper' whose beat covered Oldham's Hollins Road noticed that there always seemed to be a light on inside house number 412, the home of Joe and Jenny Mellor. He passed on his suspicions to Emma Chadwick and in due course she contacted the police with her own suspicions.

Jenny Mellor had been missing for six weeks when, on Wednesday 19 October, detectives ordered a thorough search of the house on Hollins Road and found a body concealed beneath the staircase. Although the body was in a state of decay, an autopsy was able to confirm that she had been stabbed to death and her throat cut from ear to ear.

Before Mr Justice Bruce at Manchester Assizes in November, Mellor's defence was that the police had failed to establish sufficiently the identity of the body found at the house. The prosecution claimed that Mellor had been having a relationship with a woman named Lizzie Sutherland for several years and they had even planned a date for their wedding.

Joseph Mellor. (T.J. Leech Archive)

They claimed that Mellor had committed murder in order to be free of his wife, and although the evidence against him was entirely circumstantial, it was nonetheless enough to secure a conviction.

Mellor was hanged by James Billington, making his first visit to Strangeways, on a cold Tuesday morning in December. By coincidence it was also the very day Mellor and Miss Sutherland had set for their wedding.

24

FATE BE A LESSON

Victor Emmanuel Hamer, 28 November 1893

Now all young men take a warning, and don't be led astray to drink, for the past I am sure you never can recall. While young your life enjoy, take a lesson from poor Hamer, let his fate be a lesson to you all.

Extract from 'A Murderer's Grave', a poem written by Victor Hamer while awaiting execution.

It was shortly after 6 p.m., Saturday 28 October 1893, and William Denson was settling down for his evening meal when he heard a loud bang coming from next door. Denson's neighbour on London Street, Salford, was 74-year-old Catherine Tyrer, and thinking that the elderly widow may have suffered a fall he hurried next door to investigate.

Unable to open the front door he was joined by other neighbours, who began to shout, asking the old lady if she was all right. Then a man called out that there was nothing to worry about. This aroused suspicion, and the neighbours demanded to be let in. Denson then hurried around the back and found a young man closing the back door behind him. Denson shouted for him to stop, only for the man to turn on his heel and flee.

Salford murderer Victor Hamer penned a poignant poem as he awaited execution.
(T.J. Leech Archive)

The pursuit lasted less than a minute before Denson managed to corner the man – who then pulled out a knife and waved it at him.

'Can you fight?' he taunted, thrusting the blade forward several times, all the while eying an escape route. Twenty-five-year-old Denson was not easily scared. He was able to knock the knife from the man's hand and detained him while another neighbour contacted the police.

Back inside the house the body of Mrs Tyrer was found lying in a pool of blood and she died in hospital from massive head injuries later that day.

The attacker told police his name was Victor Hamer, a 33-year-old painter, and he had been one of a gang of workmen working on the small row of terraced houses in Salford, which included those of Denson and Mrs Tyrer.

Victor Hamer stood trial at Manchester Assizes before Mr Justice Grantham on 10 December. No motive was ever clearly established for the violent attack, although police suspected that he had gone to the house to commit robbery and was surprised by the victim, whom he then pushed down the stairs. Neighbours said that for several days the victim had supplied the workmen with hot water for their tea break, but had made it clear she didn't like Hamer because she thought he was crude and roughly spoken.

Hamer blamed his plight on drink, saying that he had consumed eight pints of beer before he committed the murder and that he had no recollection of entering the house. He claimed he was not responsible for his actions and his counsel asked for a verdict of manslaughter to be brought in, due to his drunkenness.

This was rejected and the repentant Hamer penned a poignant poem as he awaited the hangman, blaming his predicament on drink and warning that his fate should be a lesson to others to be wary of the perils of alcohol. He was hanged one month to the day after committing the brutal murder.

25

THE LAST SUPPER

William Crossley, 31 July 1894

In 1892, William Crossley, a labourer at Butterworth and Dickinson's iron foundry, had taken lodgings in a large cottage at 17 Lomas Street, Burnley, with 54-year-old Mary Ann Allen and five other tenants. Mrs Allen was separated from her husband and soon began a relationship with 42-year-old Crossley.

In September 1893, Mrs Allen's daughter, Mrs Annie Robinson, and her husband, Adam, came to live with them, and from then on the atmosphere in the house changed. Relations between Crossley and his landlady became strained and, following a number of quarrels, he was told to find alternative lodgings.

On the morning of 11 June 1894, Crossley decided not to go into work, and for breakfast he drank two pints of beer. Mrs Allen came into the kitchen and they began another disagreement. Tired of the constant rows she told him firmly that he was to find fresh lodgings immediately and that his supper that night would be his last in the house.

Later that morning Crossley left Lomas Street, but at 12.45 p.m. he returned in time for his lunch. No sooner had he taken his seat than Mrs Allen reminded him that he must find new lodgings by tomorrow. Without speaking, Crossley rose from his chair and left the room. A fellow lodger saw him head in the direction of the cellar and moments later he returned to the dining room concealing something inside his coat. Crossley took his place at the table, and when Mrs Allen went into the kitchen to fetch the meal, he followed her, and attacked her with an axe. Hearing the sounds of a struggle, tenant Robert Chadwick rushed into the kitchen and tried to disarm him while another tenant ushered the young children to safety. With Mary Allen lying dead on the floor, Crossley turned on Chadwick and began to attack him before venting his anger on Mary's daughter who received serious (but not fatal) wounds.

William Crossley. (T.J. Leech Archive)

With his anger sated, Crossley dropped the axe to the ground and made his way to the nearby Waterloo Hotel, where he spotted a former employer, Councillor Dickinson, to whom he confessed his crime. He then ordered a drink and waited for the police to arrive.

At his trial before Mr Justice Bruce at Manchester Assizes on 12 June, Crossley made no attempt to deny his guilt and told friends he was prepared to face whatever punishment awaited him.

26

'ALL THROUGH A GAY LIFE'

James Wilshaw Whitehead, 27 November 1894

James Whitehead had married Mary Ann Keele in the autumn of 1887, and for a time they lived happily together on the outskirts of Oldham, becoming the parents of a young daughter, Clara. However, by 1892 relations between them had deteriorated, and several times they parted.

By the summer of 1894, 28-year-old Whitehead was working as a blind-maker and the situation between husband and wife was still fraught. Whitehead doted over his daughter and repeatedly begged his wife for them to be together again as a family. During the wakes holiday he met up with her and asked if she would reconsider his requests to get back together, adding that he had found a furnished farmhouse in Hollinwood he wanted the family to move to. She refused his pleas and the meeting ended with him making threats against her if she didn't change her mind.

On Saturday night, 25 August, Mary, her brother, and Whitehead's sister, Mrs Thomas, had been out drinking in Oldham when they spotted Whitehead as they made their way home. His sister spotted him first and said, 'Oh look, there's brother' as he approached.

No sooner had he reached them than he took out his knife, grabbed hold of his wife and cut her throat. He then fled the scene and returned home.

James Wilshaw Whitehead poses with his beloved daughter Clara. (T.J. Leech Archive)

Mary Whitehead was escorted to a doctor's surgery a few doors away and Dr Martland roused from his bed. He tried to stem the blood flow, but the wound was severe and she died from her injuries within the hour.

Police officers went to Whitehead's house and found that he had a self-inflicted throat wound and that his clothes were soaking wet. He told them that he made a failed attempt to drown himself in the nearby Crabtree Mill Lodge. He asked if his wife was dead, and when told she was, he said, 'This is all through a gay life.'

His defence at his trial before Mr Justice Kennedy on Saturday 10 November was that he was insane at the time of committing the murder. The prosecution countered this by claiming that it was premeditated murder committed because his wife refused his attempts at reconciliation.

A petition of almost 40,000 signatures collected locally failed to sway the Home Secretary into granting a reprieve and on a cold Tuesday morning in November he was hanged by James Billington. The executioner gave him a long drop of 8ft, the force of which reopened the self-inflicted neck wound, spraying the walls of the pit with blood.

27

A THING SO BAD

Joseph Hirst, 4 August 1896

On Saturday afternoon, 4 April 1896, two young boys finished their game of football on waste ground off Ashton Old Road, Openshaw. As they made their way home along Fairfield Road they stopped to wash their muddy boots in the nearby canal and discovered the body of a young girl partly submerged in the murky water. They hurried home and immediately alerted the police.

An inquest found that the child had probably been in the water just a couple of days and was aged between three or four months. Cause of death was strangulation from a piece of cord still knotted around the neck. She had been fully clothed and fastened around her waist was a heavy piece of granite, which the killer had seemingly hoped would keep the body submerged beneath the water.

Just a week earlier two children had been found in a similar condition in the River Thames – including the cord around their necks – and the police had just arrested 57-year-old grandmother Amelia Dyer. Dyer would eventually be suspected of the murder of seven or eight children, and although it was initially believed the two cases may be linked, she was soon eliminated from these enquiries.

The story was reported in the local papers and a woman came forward who recognised the clothing as belonging to the child of her neighbours Joseph Hirst and Martha Ann Goddard. Detectives discovered that Hirst, a 26-year-old bricklayer, and 20-year-old Goddard had lived together as man and wife in lodgings in Chorlton-on-Medlock since December of the previous year and she had given birth to a daughter they called Maud in January. Following the birth they had moved to new lodgings and on 2 April the couple left the house carrying the child, telling their landlady they were taking her to be cared for by Hirst's mother.

Hirst's mother was traced to Stockport and told detectives that although she had looked after the child in the past they had not left the child with her. A hunt for the missing couple lasted six weeks and took detectives across Lancashire to Nottinghamshire, to Derby and finally on to Leicester where they were apprehended.

As the couple were returned to Manchester for questioning it was clear to detectives that the woman lived in fear of the short, stocky, fiery redhead Hirst, who was known to have a violent temper. The woman had bruises to her face and a medical examination found she had extensive bruises on her legs and body. She told detectives that Hirst would beat and threaten her on a regular basis and on occasions forced her to work as a prostitute.

Hirst was so sure of the hold he had over her that he believed she wouldn't testify against him, but once officers convinced her she had nothing to fear from him, she made a detailed statement, saying that he had told her he didn't want the burden of the child and how he had strangled Maud and then thrown her into the canal.

This testimony formed the basis of the prosecution's evidence when Hirst appeared at Manchester Assizes on 14 July before trial judge Mr Commissioner Dugdale QC. Although Goddard was to be charged as an accessory, the prosecution offered no evidence against her and she was discharged.

Following conviction Hirst admitted that he had strangled the child after he had become tired of it crying and told a friend he did not expect a reprieve after committing a thing so bad.

28

'SOMETHING I NEVER DONE'

George Howe, 22 February 1898

George Howe fully accepted he should pay with his life for his crime, but he was equally determined he would not face the hangman. Following conviction he told friends he would starve himself to death rather than walk to the gallows, and for a time he tried to carry out his threat.

Thirty-three-year-old Howe lived with his wife and three children on Clarence Street in Burnley, and during the autumn of 1897 he was employed at Messrs Brooks and Pickup brickworks adjacent to Towneley colliery and railway station. Sometime during November an incident occurred involving his wages, which resulted in Howe being dismissed. Howe vehemently denied the charges and made a number of visits to the brickworks to try to resolve the matter. On his final visit he was told it was now too late to do anything about it as someone else had been employed in his position.

Howe was forced to take a job at Reedley Colliery, a fair distance from his home, and not only did it entail a long journey to and from work each day, but the wages were much less than what he had been earning at the brickworks. He insisted to anyone who would listen that he had been dismissed for 'something I never done' and made a number of threats that he would 'swing for Jack Pickup.'

John 'Jack' Keirby Pickup was the 56-year-old manager at the brickworks and it was he that Howe blamed for his dismissal, although it appears that Pickup had tried to get Howe reinstated but was overruled by another manager.

Early on the morning of New Year's Eve, Jack Pickup was found slumped beside a level crossing close to the brickworks. One of his daily tasks was to walk the short distance down the railway line connecting the brickworks to the colliery checking the condition of the track. He had been beaten with a heavy stick, struck about the head with his lantern and then kicked several times in the face.

Jack Kirkup – murdered by George Howe at Burnley. (T.J. Leech Archive)

Warders prevented killer George Howe starving himself to death so that 'the law could take its course'. (T.J. Leech Archive)

Howe immediately confessed to attacking Pickup and was taken into custody charged with grievous bodily harm. His clothes were examined and traces of blood were found on his clothes and engrained in the leather of his clogs. Pickup was taken to hospital, where initially he seemed to be recovering from his injuries – unfortunately, however, this recovery was short lived, and a week later he died.

Howe was then charged with murder and appeared before Mr Justice Wills at Manchester Assizes on 3 February 1898. The case was a formality: Howe had already admitted assaulting Pickup and was therefore responsible for his death. It only needed the matter of deciding whether he was guilty of murder or manslaughter, and since Howe had been known to have a grievance against the dead man, and to have made threats against him, it took the jury less than an hour to find him guilty of murder.

Howe collapsed in tears when the verdict was returned and was sobbing so loudly he was unable to reply when asked if he had anything to say as to why sentence of death should not be passed on him. Once he was taken to the cells he recovered his composure and told his wife and friends that he planned to cheat the hangman and refuse any kind of food. The prison authorities would have none of this, and Howe was removed to the prison hospital where he was force-fed to keep him alive until he made his 8 p.m. appointment with Billington and son.

29

A BROKEN PROMISE

Michael Dowdle, 6 December 1899

Michael Dowdle was a 40-year-old Irish-born ex-soldier who had served gallantly with the 18th Royal Irish Regiment in the Zulu War. After he was pensioned off, he returned to live with his 36-year-old wife Ellen and their five children in the family home on Copeland Street, Whitworth, near Rochdale.

In the summer of 1899, while he was working as a quarryman, his wife left him due to his increasingly quarrelsome and brutal behaviour. On 12 August, she went to stay with friends, Mr and Mrs O'Brien, who lived nearby on Grove Terrace. Dowdle made repeated requests for Ellen to come back to him, but each request fell on deaf ears.

On 19 August, Dowdle called at Grove Terrace and found his wife alone. He made a passionate plea for her to return home and promised to mend his ways. She told him she would consider it, but she was scared that he would beat her if she did. He promised he would not, and asked her to accompany him back that afternoon. She finally agreed and they set off back to Copeland Street.

No sooner had they returned than they began to quarrel and her worst fears were confirmed: Dowdle broke the promise he had made not to beat her. In fact, he turned on her with dreadful violence: first, he kicked her to the floor – and then he pulled out his knife and cut her throat. Her screams brought neighbours to the door, but Dowdle's fearsome reputation meant that no one was brave enough to confront him. Instead a child climbed onto the window sill, spied what was happening behind the door and rushed down the street shouting for help, 'Come quick, Mr Dowdle is hacking up his wife's throat with a carving knife!'

Eventually a policeman was found, and when he reached the house, Dowdle, resigned to his fate, was already walking towards the police station, followed by a crowd of children. A doctor had also been called to the house, but by the time he arrived Ellen Dowdle had died from her injuries. As well as the fearful kicking she had received, her throat had been deeply cut, close to her right ear.

Dowdle stood trial before Mr Justice Kennedy at Manchester Assizes on 17 November. His defence was that he was insane and evidence was heard that he had left the army after contracting sunstroke in South Africa, which had rendered him prone to blackouts. He had also

How The Illustrated Police News *recorded Michael Dowdle's murder of his wife.* (T.J. Leech Archive)

suffered severe head injuries in a fall at the quarry earlier that spring. The prosecution claimed that Dowdle had killed his wife because she had left him – and presumably had told him shortly before her death that she wanted to end their marriage. Friends at Grove Terrace claimed she had told them this is what she had planned. Coupled with the threats they told police Dowdle had made against his wife, this was enough to convince the jury he was guilty of wilful murder and not insane. The jury added a strong recommendation for mercy, which the judge said he would forward to the appropriate quarters. But it was to be in vain, and Michael Dowdle became the last man to be hanged in the nineteenth century

30

THE EVIL GRANDFATHER

Joseph Holden, 4 December 1900

Fifty-seven-year-old Joseph Holden had gone through a stressful few months. His wife, and the mother of his eleven children, had suddenly passed away in the summer of 1900 and Holden had taken her death badly. He had always been fond of a drink or two, but as a result of heavy drinking, his work as an iron turner at an engineering factory began to suffer. His boss, aware of his recent bereavement, initially tolerated the odd day off, brought on by the drink, but when it became a regular habit he had no choice but to give Holden the sack.

From that moment Holden set off on a path that was lead to the gallows before the year had ended. Soon after his dismissal from work he found himself homeless, which led to him having to take up lodgings at the Bury Workhouse.

At the beginning of August he called on one of his daughters, a Mrs Dawes, who had a house in Nuttall Street, Bury, and moved in with her until her husband, who was working away from home, returned. While he was pleased to escape the squalid workhouse conditions, Holden was nonetheless angry that she could only offer him temporary lodgings and as a result they frequently quarrelled. Despite the rows, however, she was reluctant to turn him out onto the streets.

Two weeks after moving in he visited another of his daughters, Mrs Eldred, who lived a few streets away. When he reached her house he spotted her 9-year-old son, George, playing in the street outside. Holden asked his grandson if he would like to go for a walk with him but the boy declined, but when he promised him two pigeons if he would accompany him to the quarry, the young lad quickly changed his mind and they set off down the road together.

A short time later young George was telling his horrified parents that Granddad Joe had struck him on the head with a stone while he was cutting some tobacco. He related how he had been offered the pigeons and that, after striking him, Granddad had bandaged the wound and put him on the tram for home.

In a rage, George's mother rushed round to confront her father, but found him quietly eating his tea. He told her that boy had simply fallen. The family doctor who tended the wound said he doubted that the boy could have sustained the cut by falling, but there was no evidence to suggest otherwise. As a result the family decided not to inform the police and treated the matter as an unfortunate accident.

Less than a fortnight later, on 5 September, Holden walked into a local police station and confessed to the murder of his grandson John Dawes. The body of the 8-year-old was found in a quarry at Limefield, Bury. Holden said he had thrown the boy down onto some rocks in the quarry. He said he had then made his way down into the quarry and, finding the boy still alive, he picked him up and threw him into some water. A post-mortem found that the cause of death was due to drowning.

Grandfather Joseph Holden.
(T.J. Leech Archive)

At Manchester Assizes before Mr Justice Darling on 4 December, Holden pleaded guilty to the charge of murder. His defence claimed that Holden was insane and not fit to plead, but following a review by the prison medical board the plea was allowed to stand and Holden was sentenced to death.

31

OLD FRIENDS

Patrick McKenna, 3 December 1901

The Derby Hotel on Churchgate, run by hangman James Billington, was a popular drinking hostelry for people living in the Haulgh and town-centre regions of Bolton. The bars were popular with customers who frequented the adjacent theatres as well as local men who regularly occupied the taproom, one of whom was Patrick McKenna, a 53-year-old joiner, who lived on nearby Kestor Street.

McKenna and his wife Ann had to take in lodgers, Mr and Mrs Palmer, when he lost his job, and McKenna soon became suspicious that his wife was having an affair with Palmer. Despite McKenna finding work as a labourer he continued to drink heavily and was often short of money as he regularly took days off work.

On Sunday 27 September 1901, McKenna was drunk again and did not go to work the following day. That afternoon Ann spent the day with her daughter-in-law. McKenna followed her there and asked for some money, but she refused to give him any. He was furious, and as he left he threatened to cut her head off before the end of the day.

Later that same day McKenna entered the house and dragged his wife from the kitchen, where she had been hiding, and into the front room. He then picked up a knife from the table and plunged it into her neck, at the same time accusing her of taking a cup of tea to the lodger Palmer that morning. Ann died within a few minutes in the arms of one of the neighbours. McKenna was taken into custody, but he could not be charged until the following morning as he was so drunk.

At his trial on 13 November, his defence claimed that McKenna was greatly depressed as he could only find work as a labourer, and that, as he had been under the influence of alcohol at the time of the murder, he was unable to form any intention to kill his wife and the murder charge should be amended to manslaughter. The jury returned a verdict of guilty of murder.

James Billington, the landlord of his local pub, and someone he had come to regard as a friend over the years, carried out McKenna's execution. Their families were well known to each other, and indeed Billington's son William was one of the people that had attended to McKenna's wife while she lay dying following the attack.

James Billington had been in poor health in the days leading up the execution, but he was determined to carry out his duties as requested. He was to be assisted by newly qualified assistant Henry Pierrepoint. Once they had reached the prison and prepared the drop, Billington returned to his quarters quite distressed and told his assistant that he wished he had not made the journey after all.

The following morning McKenna walked to his death showing great penitence and sobbing loudly. It would be Billington's last execution: ten days later he passed away. Friends at the Derby Arms claimed it was as a result of leaving his sickbed to hang his old friend.

Hangman James Billington left his sickbed to execute his friend Patrick McKenna (right). It was Billington's last execution and he died a few days later. (Both Author's Collection)

Bolton-born Harry Mack was hanged by the country's new chief executioner William Billington (right) who had taken over from his father. (T.J. Leech Archive and Author's Collection)

32

NO MERCY

Henry McWiggins, 2 December 1902

Although christened Henry McWiggins, the 29-year-old Bolton-born fireman was known to friends and workmates simply as Harry Mack. Since June 1902 Mack was living in lodgings at 22 Hopwood Street, Oldham, with 32-year-old Esther Redford, and although they had initially been on friendly terms, things soon deteriorated.

Several times in August their landlady, a Mrs Haigh, heard sounds of a violent disturbance going on in the room. On the first occasion, on the evening of Saturday 2 August, she found Mack dragging Esther across the floor by her hair. She screamed at him to stop, and when he let go of her hair he slapped and kicked her before storming out of the house. It should have been a warning to the unfortunate woman, but she ignored the landlady's suggestion to consider leaving Mack.

One week later Mack was served a meal prepared by Esther and complained to both her and the landlady that the meal seemed to contain just potatoes and very little meat. When Esther collected the empty dishes and went into the kitchen, Mack followed her and attacked her, blacking both eyes and kicking her as she slumped to the ground.

The brutality continued on the following day when Mack woke Esther by kicking her out of bed; the day ended with him striking her in the face with a shovel. Both the landlady and another lodger who had witnessed the violent assaults warned her to tell the police, but she seemed to be too terror-stricken to do so.

The following day, Monday 11 August, Mack's violent assaults escalated. Following sounds of a scuffle going on upstairs, Mrs Haigh heard loud screams coming from Mack's room and, rushing to investigate, she found Esther lying on the bed, her face blistered badly after Mack had thrown a kettle full of boiling water at her. Still she refused to call the police, and when Mack returned that night he immediately launched another assault against her, slapping her around the face so hard that the newly formed blisters burst. He then kicked and jumped on her prone body. This time the landlady took it upon herself to intervene and called the police.

Esther Redford was taken to the local infirmary, where it was discovered that her injuries included a ruptured bladder. With Mack in custody Esther was persuaded to testify against him. However, despite her horrific injuries, she was either too much in love or too terrified to speak against him, and so she claimed that she had fallen, and the burns to her face had been caused when she accidentally spilled the kettle. She died from her injuries the following day.

Despite Esther's testimony to the contrary, police believed that Harry Mack had murdered her and he stood trial at Manchester Assizes on 14 November. Evidence was heard by a number of doctors who had examined the victim. They each claimed her extensive injuries were the result of a fearful beating, and landlady Mrs Haigh told the court of the assaults she had witnessed at her home.

The defence chose to focus on the dying woman's testimony and also claimed that descriptions of both the injuries and the attacks had been greatly exaggerated by the witnesses.

On the second day, with evidence completed, trial judge Mr Justice Jelf told the jury that they must be satisfied there was great violence inflicted if they were to return a verdict of guilty of murder. If they didn't believe there was they would have to acquit the prisoner. There were only two possible verdicts: guilty or not guilty of murder. It took them twenty minutes to decide on the former. Passing sentence, the judge told Mack, an ex-criminal with a long list of convictions – and described in the press as 'a veritable pest' – to expect no mercy.

33

BAD BLOOD

William George Hudson, 12 May 1903

It was while they were stationed at Fulwood Barracks, Preston, that Bombardier Harry Short made an official complaint against his comrade William George Hudson, a 26-year-old gunner in the 7th Depot Royal Field Artillery, following a breach of military discipline. Bombardier Short reported him to a senior officer, and although charges against Birmingham-born Hudson were subsequently dropped, Hudson swore that he would get even with Short. From then on the situation between the two men became so tense that they were billeted in different parts of the camp and kept apart as much as possible.

On the night of 16 February 1903, Hudson and two friends left the barracks for a night of heavy drinking. As they returned to their quarters Hudson became aggressive and began shouting he wanted to get even with Short. He staggered out of his room and tried to make his way to Short's quarters, only to be stopped from entering and taken to his own room. Hudson slumped onto his bunk and a friend helped him out of his boots and tried to convince him to go to sleep. A short time later he got out of bed and took a cartridge from his box before entering an adjacent room, where he took down a rifle belonging to another soldier.

The following morning Short was found dead in his bed, a bullet having entered below his chin and penetrated his brain. Hudson was the immediate suspect and an inquiry soon found he had fired the fatal shot, and he was charged with murder.

He stood trial before Mr Justice Lawrence at Manchester Assizes on 24 April. The prosecution's case was based mainly on circumstantial evidence, as no one had seen the crime committed and there was no direct evidence pointing to Hudson beyond the bad blood that had existed between him and Short, and the fact that he had previously been heard making threats against Bombardier Short.

After only a short deliberation the jury found him guilty of murder, but adding a strong recommendation to mercy on account of his previous good character. Hudson declared his innocence when the judge asked if he had anything to say before sentence was passed.

34

THE COLLYHURST MURDER

Charles Wood Whittaker, 2 December 1903

Eliza Range had been separated from her husband for the best part of fifteen years, since shortly after the birth of her son, but by the turn of the century they attempted reconciliation. It was soon clear that any romance had long gone, and although they shared the same house it was more for convenience than love, and each was free to see other people.

Home was at 99 Husband Street, Collyhurst, and by spring 1903, 43-year-old Eliza was involved in a relationship with Charlie Whittaker, a 43-year-old casual labourer who worked in the

Lancashire and Yorkshire Railway's goods yard off the Oldham Road. Eliza's husband also worked for the railway, but the two men had different shifts, and most days Whittaker would call round at Husband Street, where he and Eliza would get drunk.

On the morning of 8 August 1903, Eliza's son Arthur was having breakfast while his mother and Whittaker were drinking beer in the kitchen. Suddenly Eliza announced she was going to take a wash, and after refilling Whittaker's glass she rose from her chair and walked towards the scullery. Arthur saw Whittaker follow her, clutching a knife, but before he could react Whittaker had pushed Eliza into a corner, and moments later she let out a fearful scream. As Arthur rushed to his mother's aid, Whittaker fled from the house. Eliza lay bleeding to death on the scullery floor from four stab wounds, one that had cut her throat so deeply that an artery had been severed, and by the time a doctor could be summoned Eliza Range was dead.

The following day Whittaker surrendered to the police, having read in the morning paper that Eliza had died. 'I'm the man who committed the murder yesterday,' he announced to the desk sergeant, and when the officer looked sceptically at him, and scrutinised a picture of the wanted man, Whittaker confirmed it was indeed him. 'You needn't look at that, it's me alright. I'd have come sooner only I wanted a drink!'

When he stood trial before Mr Justice Ridley at Manchester Assizes on 9 November, the prosecution offered a motive for the crime and claimed that Eliza Range earned a small income cleaning for a neighbour. Although he knew she was married and shared a bed with her husband, he also knew it was a loveless relationship, which Whittaker was comfortable with. However, he was jealous of the neighbour and had tried, unsuccessfully, to stop her working for this man. The longer she continued the angrier he had become, until he finally snapped. Following his arrest Whittaker made a statement to the effect that Eliza had been unfaithful to him, but there was no proof in that claim.

His defence suggested that at the time of the attack, Whittaker had been so mad with drink and rage that he had temporarily lost his senses. The jury rejected his defence, and as he passed sentence Mr Justice Ridley told him that he could entertain no hope of a reprieve.

Charles Whittaker's execution marked the debut as chief executioner of John Billington, son of James and youngest of the three Billington brothers.

35

'NO' BUT TO DIE THE ONCE ... '

John Griffiths, 27 February 1906

Sunday Feb 25th 1906
Dear Mother and Father and Sisters and Brothers,

I write these few lines hoping to find you all in good health and the best of spirits. Dear Mother, I must tell you that the Governor came this morning to tell me that the Home Secretary can see no grounds for a reprieve and that I must prepare to meet my God which I am hoping to do. I hope that you will try and forgive me and forget me for what I have done. I hope that you will see Mr Butterworth, my solicitor, and all who have been doing their best for me, and I hope you will tell the Winterburn family that I send them my best love. I also hope that you will send word to our Lizzie and Willie that I am very sorry that they cannot come and see me. Tell my brothers and sisters from me that I hope they will try for a better life than I have done. I hope you will tell Mr and Mrs Schofield that I send them my best love.

Kate Geraghty and John Griffiths (right). (T.J. Leech Archive)

I am very glad to tell you that I have had plenty of good books to read since I have been in prison and they have been very good books. They have cheered me up and I have had them sent in by the prison chaplain. He has made me happier than I have been before in my life and I have been taking notice of all he has been saying. He has been reading the Bible and praying for me every day and I have been wishing I had looked after myself and gone to Sunday school on Sundays. I hope that you will keep sending our Mary and Janie and George to Sunday school and don't let our George lead the same life as me. If he doesn't go to Sunday school when you send him, take him the Sunday after. I hope you will tell our Bob and Charlie from me that I hope they will try and keep out of bad company, and all my mates too, and tell John Thomas Dignan that I send him my best respects.

Dear Mother I hope that you will have that medal of mine made into a broach for my sake. I hope that we shall meet in the next world and I hope that when I leave this world for the next I shall meet my Loving Katie. I will ask her to forgive me and I hope that she will do so. I think that this is all at present.

From your loving son
John Griffiths
P.S. I forgot to tell you that the Governor has treated me very kind and allowed me to write a letter when I want it, and I have been looked after very well since I have been in here and I have been allowed tobacco and a pipe to smoke, so good afternoon.

The winter's evening of 19 December 1905 had already drawn in when 17-year-old Catherine 'Katie' Geraghty left her parents' home at Shaw to fetch a jug of ale for the family to drink with supper. She never returned. Her worried parents made a frantic search, but could not find her. The following morning her body was found when a man making his way to work stumbled across her corpse lying covered in sacking, on frozen wasteland well away from the busy road close by. She had been strangled with a piece of string.

Police investigating what was clearly a case of murder soon had a prime suspect in 19-year-old John Griffiths, a neighbour of Katie's. (By coincidence, it had been Griffiths' father who had found the body.)

Griffiths and Katie had been sweethearts, but recently they had fallen out, and at the time of her murder she wasn't on speaking terms with him. This had stemmed from an incident two weeks earlier when Griffiths, returning home from his shift in the local mill, spotted Katie talking to a young man on the corner of the street. It was an innocent chance meeting, but enough to drive Griffiths into a rage.

'What's going on here then?' he shouted, and without waiting for an answer, Griffiths launched himself at the other man, handing out a fierce beating, until the screaming Katie dragged him off. For Katie this was the last straw. She had already forgiven him for striking her a few weeks previously following another jealous quarrel, but seeing the ferociousness of the beating, she decided to end the relationship for good.

Linking Griffiths to the crime was a simple matter. Witnesses came forward who had seen Katie talking to him on the corner of Greenfield Lane at around 8.15 p.m. on the night she disappeared and a trail of footprints left in the sodden earth, which trailed away from the body in the direction of the nearby mill, proved a perfect match to Griffiths' boots.

John Griffiths stood trial before Mr Justice Grantham at Manchester Assizes the following February. He pleaded not guilty to the charge and showed a callous disregard to the whole proceedings. The case against him was strong – the footprints and the eyewitness accounts being particularly telling. The judge's summing up left no one in any doubt as to what he thought the verdict should be; the jury concurred, and on 6 February, the second day of the trial, they needed just a short time to find him guilty. As sentence was passed on him he turned to the judge and declared, 'I've no'but to die the once', before leaving the dock with a smile.

Griffiths continued to plead his innocence, but shortly before he was to die it appeared his conscience got the better of him and he made a full confession. Griffiths was hanged by Henry Pierrepoint, and the vastly experienced hangman later recalled that Griffiths had shown no sign of fear or false bravado as he walked to the gallows. 'He was the youngest man I hanged, and one of the bravest.'

36

THIS TERRIBLE FATE

John Ramsbottom, 12 May 1908

Early in the new year of 1908, 34-year-old John Ramsbottom called into a Manchester gunsmith's and attempted to buy a revolver. The shopkeeper asked to see a firearm certificate, and when Ramsbottom was unable to produce the required paperwork, the shopkeeper told him he was not permitted to sell him a gun. Undaunted, Ramsbottom left the shop. A few days later, having acquired the relevant documents, he returned, and was allowed to purchase a revolver and bullets.

On Thursday evening, 20 February, Ramsbottom visited his estranged wife, Charlotte, and their child, at her mother's home in Gorton. The Ramsbottoms had married in October 1907, shortly before the birth of their first child, but within just a few months they had parted. The marriage had ended when Charlotte Ramsbottom discovered that her husband had a drinking problem; she also suspected he was having an affair. Taking their young baby, Charlotte went to stay with her mother, the licensee of The Prince of Wales on Abbey Hey Lane, Gorton. Although they no longer lived together, Charlotte and her husband remained friends, and Ramsbottom would frequently spend the night at the pub.

Around midnight a quarrel started between them, rising to such a level that Charlotte's mother and brother James came rushing to the bedroom to see what was going on. A shot rang out. Entering the bedroom they discovered Charlotte lying on the bed suffering from a bullet wound to the left breast, while Ramsbottom stood in the doorway brandishing his gun. The baby lay asleep and unharmed in a cot by the side of the mother's bed. A further shot was fired, bursting a water pipe, before Ramsbottom pointed the gun at his brother-in-law, with whom he had previously been friendly. He fired twice; the first bullet missed, but the second hit him in the stomach, killing him instantly. With the gun in his hand and dressed only in his nightshirt, Ramsbottom rushed out into the street and made for his mother's house, where he was arrested soon after.

In the dock at Manchester Assizes on 22 April, Ramsbottom was charged with the wilful murder of James McCraw and the attempted murder of his wife. The prosecution tried to prove that it was a premeditated attack, based mainly on the testimony of the gunsmith who sold Ramsbottom the gun.

His defence chose the only option open to them – that he was guilty but insane – but he was duly found guilty of murder and sentenced to death. A petition for a reprieve was arranged and some 25,000 signatures were collected (although many signed out of sympathy for Ramsbottom's mother, an elderly and much-admired member of the community, devastated by the tragedy). The petition failed to sway the Home Secretary and his appeal was also rejected. From his cell he sent a message to his workmates, warning them 'that drink was his downfall' and to take 'this terrible fate' as a warning.

37

ONE AND SIX FOR BLACKPOOL

Fred Ballington, 28 July 1908

It was in the late spring of 1908 that Ann Ballington finally lost patience with her husband and, with the aid of her son, threw him out of the family home. Drink had been the problem for 41-year-old Fred Ballington, to the extent that he lost his job as a butcher in his hometown of Glossop, Derbyshire, and following his dismissal he sought consolation in a variety of local hostelries until his wife had had enough.

Ballington moved to Manchester, taking lodgings in Hulme, and set about trying to win his wife back. It was not successful and every effort and gesture was knocked back. He made several attempts to get her to arrange a meeting. She finally agreed, but when she refused to take him back he decided on drastic action.

On 25 May 1908, they met up in Manchester and he again asked her for a second chance. Again she refused, and as she made to return home Ballington followed her to London Road station where she would catch a train to Glossop. As they waited on the platform they argued yet again. At 5.20 p.m. Ann's train arrived and she boarded, followed closely by her husband.

Ann was in a crowded compartment and Ballington asked her to move to a quieter part of the train. She refused, and their raised voices attracted the attention of other travellers. 'We've done all the talking we're going to do,' she said coldly. Ballington realised that all his hopes of reconciliation had been in vain and this was the end. He asked her for some money, enough to go to Blackpool where he hoped to find a job.

'All the money you've ever had has been wasted down the drain,' she told him, then seemed to relent and opened her purse. Carefully she counted a number of coins and handed them over.

'One and six!' Ballington exclaimed, 'That's no use to me.' Told that was all he was getting, he seemed to accept something was better than nothing and headed for the carriage door, before pausing and addressing his wife: 'I'll say goodbye then.'

She refused his request for a farewell kiss and instead of continuing his exit he stood firm and spoke again: 'Now it is goodbye, and goodbye for ever!' And at that, Ballington pulled out a knife, rushed towards her and stabbed her in throat, before turning the knife on himself.

Ann Ballington died on the carriage floor, but Ballington's wounds were minor and he was patched up in time for his trial at Manchester Assizes before Mr Justice Bucknill on 7 July. With a carriage full of witnesses there was no doubt that Ballington was guilty of killing his wife. Admitting his guilt Ballington said, 'I had done it, all through 1s 6d for Blackpool. The sooner they hang me the better.'

By the time Ballington came to trial a new law came into force that allowed condemned prisoners the chance of an appeal against their sentence, but Ballington was resigned to his fate and chose not to take this historic step, and three weeks later he calmly walked to the gallows.

38

'ONE LIFE FOR THE PRICE OF TWO!'

Mark Shawcross, 3 August 1909

Although still married, 27-year-old Emily Ramsbottom had separated from her husband and for three tempestuous years had been living with Mark Shawcross, a 30-year-old labourer from Gorton. She bore him two children but, following a series of drunken quarrels, in the summer of 1908 she decided that it would be wiser to take the children and move back in with her mother. Emily and Shawcross seemed to be trying to mend the relationship and she and the children often spent long periods living with Shawcross. They talked about moving back in together and gradually most of her things were returned to Shawcross's home.

In May 1909, following another argument, Emily moved out again; collecting her things, she told him their relationship was over. Despite his pleadings she refused to return home, but, on the evening of Wednesday 12 May, she agreed to his request to meet up and go to the theatre. Later that evening they were seen walking together seeming happy enough. The following morning the body of Emily Ramsbottom was found in a nearby field, her handkerchief fastened round her neck in a reef knot. Shawcross could not be found.

Then, three days later, detectives received an anonymous letter. It contained a confession to the murder of Emily Ramsbottom and declared, 'I killed her with my bare hands and as quickly as possible. She was almost dead when I tied the handkerchief round her neck . . .'

After being on the run for almost a week, tired and exhausted, Shawcross returned home shortly before midnight on 20 May. Detectives had placed a watch on the house and once he entered they stormed inside and he was arrested.

Under interrogation he denied the murder and claimed that after leaving the cinema he had left Emily at about 11 p.m. and walked on to Todmorden where he was hoping to find work the following morning. He admitted to writing the anonymous letter to the police and another to a foreman at his former place of work in which he actually signed his name, but claimed he had done so after reading about the crime in a newspaper. Asked why he would want to confess to murder if he was innocent, Shawcross claimed he was sick and tired of life.

At the trial before Mr Justice Hamilton on 6 July, the prosecution's case was based mainly on the letters, which they suggested amounted to a written confession. Despite Shawcross's attempts to explain away the letters, and a plea by the defence that he was insane, the jury weren't convinced and duly found him guilty.

Shortly before he was hanged Shawcross acknowledged his guilt and declared that it was 'one life for the price of two!' Asked to elaborate, he confessed to his guards that he had killed a Negro while serving in South Africa and on that occasion he had escaped detection. For this second murder he was duly hanged.

39

THE FIRST PERSON HE MET

Joseph Wren, 22 February 1910

Joe Wren was 20 years old when the navy decided to dispense with his services. After an unhappy childhood which had resulted in him spending some time in prison, he took to navy life and spent many happy months at sea and greatly enjoyed his work as a stoker on a training vessel. Therefore, it was not only a shock but also a massive disappointment when he was discharged from service due to his poor eyesight.

He returned to his native Burnley and spent the best part of the next two years wandering the streets, unable to find regular employment. The situation got worse when his girlfriend became pregnant – once the child was born, he had extra responsibilities and no income. He then decided that he would murder the woman and her child, but unable to find the opportunity, on Tuesday 28 December 1909 he left home and vowed to murder the first person he would meet that day.

As he set out for town he came across his elder brother and asked him for a loan, which was refused, as was his request for a cigarette. Wren then turned to his brother and told him that he was going to go back to prison, 'this time for five or six years, even if it meant murder.' After being told to behave and to keep looking for a job, the brothers parted.

Within the hour Wren was seen by an acquaintance in the company of a small boy, 3-year-old John Collins, who Wren was leading by the hand in the direction of railway sidings at Bank Hall Pit. Wren had bumped into the boy who was walking down the street hoping to meet his mother coming home from work.

An hour later Wren walked up to a police officer and told him that he had just committed a murder. He was detained while another officer was sent to check his story. Soon the details of Wren's confession were confirmed and the horrified constable was able to report that he had found the body of a young boy with a neck wound. A post-mortem found that death had been due to strangulation before the throat was cut.

On 4 February 1910 Wren appeared before Mr Commissioner (soon to be Mr Justice) Avory at Manchester Assizes. The prosecution based its evidence on the confession to the police officer, the threat to his brother about committing murder, and letters that Wren had sent from his cell which contained details about the crime.

The defence chose the only option open to them, that Wren was insane when he committed the crime. They claimed there was hereditary insanity in the family and that Wren was an epileptic. Evidence was also cited that the prisoner had tried to commit suicide in his cell before the trial.

Little mourned and shunned by his family, Wren was hanged on a frosty February morning for a brutal and totally pointless murder.

40

ONE LAST DRINK

John Edward Tarkenter, 12 December 1911

John and Rosetta Tarkenter had married in June 1889 and for a time lived happily together. Things changed shortly after the birth of their first child; John became quarrelsome, short tempered and turned to drinking heavily. In 1892 following another quarrel he left home. He was gone for over nine years, during which time he enlisted in the army and fought bravely in South Africa.

In 1901 he returned to the family home at Heyside, Royton, and made peace with his wife. He found a job as a spinner in a mill in nearby Shaw, and for a while it seemed they were happy together again. But then the old habits returned. He hit the bottle again and in August 1910, he left his wife for the fourth time, not returning until June 1911, during which he spent a period of time in a workhouse in Preston. It was around this time that he was involved in a drunken quarrel in a public house and was severely wounded when someone smashed a bottle over his head.

Although Tarkenter had walked out on his wife for long periods of time he was nevertheless jealous at the thought that she may have been seeing other men during his absence, but although she denied that she had he made constant references to her infidelity whenever he was drunk. This last period away from home may have caused him to assess the relationship and he made efforts to cut his drinking and to improve his conduct towards his wife.

At first light on Tuesday 18 July, Tarkenter woke his eldest son, George, and while George dressed for work he could hear his parents chatting in their room amiably enough. George left for work at 5.30 a.m. and shortly afterwards a neighbour heard sounds of a disturbance and raised voices coming from Tarkenter's house. At shortly after 8 a.m. the same neighbour on his way to work saw John Tarkenter entering a nearby public house.

George Tarkenter returned home from work at 5.40 p.m. and was surprised to find the front door locked. He let himself in and found that there was no fire in the grate; neither was there any sign of tea having been cooked, and when he went upstairs he was horrified to find his mother dead in her bed in a pool of blood, her throat having been cut.

While the son rushed to call the police, John Tarkenter was finishing his drink in a Shaw public house. As he walked outside he bumped into his brother, also called George Tarkenter. He asked George to stand him a drink, as it would be, 'the last one I will have.' Asked what he meant by that Tarkenter pulled out a razor and told him, 'I have cut Rose's throat.' He refused his brother's request to go and find a policeman, but a search was already out for him when Police Sergeant Taylor spotted him on St Mary's Gate, Shaw, later that evening.

Tarkenter was swigging ale from a jug when the officer approached and he told him, 'I know you have come for me. I know I have cut her throat. I know I will have to swing for it. I will tell you what I have done with the razor if you will pay for a pint of beer.'

Told he was being arrested on suspicion of murder, Tarkenter simply replied, 'That's right; I have done it.'

At his Manchester trial on 22 November before Mr Justice Avory, Tarkenter pleaded not guilty to murder. He offered a defence of insanity and admitted killing Rosetta because she had provoked him during an argument, and suggested that he was therefore guilty only of manslaughter. The jury were not convinced and Tarkenter was sentenced to death. He made no appeal against the sentence and told friends he deserved his fate and was ready to die. He had a touching farewell interview with his son, brother and two sisters. As the meeting drew to a close, Tarkenter strongly advised his son to be a total abstainer. Saying goodbye for the last time, his son promised that he would.

41

SOMETHING SERIOUS

Walter Martyn, 12 December 1911

The silence was broken by the muted tones of the prison chaplain reciting the burial service as the procession to the gallows began. The two condemned men, who up until that moment had not met, walked close by each other the few short paces to the execution shed. Assistant hangman George Brown from Ashton-under-Lyne was feeling the strain. It was only his second execution, and at his first, a few months before, he had been lucky to escape serious injury when the condemned man gave him a hefty kick with hobnailed boots as he went to pinion him. The scene had been chaotic, with the prisoner screaming, kicking and fighting every inch to the drop. This time both prisoners had succumbed to the strapping without a word and he breathed a sigh of relief as they moved towards the drop without a struggle.

Double executions were a rarity at Manchester, with this only the second in the forty-two years since the prison opened, and as a result a large crowd had assembled outside the gates from an early hour. By 8 a.m., as the prison bell began its mournful toll, a crowd of over 300 people stood in silence as the two men paid for their crimes. Although little effort was made to secure a reprieve for John Tarkenter (see chapter 40), strenuous efforts had been made for his partner-in-death, 23-year-old Walter Martyn, who had strangled his girlfriend in a wood at Heywood.

Walter Martyn, a pot-man at the Black Bull Inn on Rochdale Road, Heywood, had known Edith Griffiths for little over a year when, in September 1911, he moved in to live with her and her stepmother at their house on Adelaide Street, Heywood. Two years before, Edith had been engaged to another man, but shortly after the birth of a child, the relationship had ended and she was left to bring up the child alone.

Martyn accepted the situation, but although she had severed all contact with her former fiancé, he was still jealous whenever his name was mentioned.

On Thursday evening, 28 September, Edith's mother Elizabeth arrived home from work at 7.30 p.m., and half an hour later Edith and Martyn went out together. They were later seen by friends walking in the direct of Plumpton Wood, in the Crimble area of town, but at 10.15 p.m., Martyn was in the Brown Cow Hotel drinking alone. He then headed back to the Black Bull where, after downing a large glass of rum, he confessed to his boss, landlord Richard Ramsbottom, that Edith was dead in Plumpton Wood, and that she had been with another man. He then went outside and finding a police officer, he said, 'I think I have done something serious', before confessing he had committed a murder.

Taken into custody Martyn made a number of conflicting statements. In one he denied anything to do with her death, but finally he admitted that he and Edith had gone for a walk, when Edith had asked him to buy her some toffee. He gave her a penny and she nipped around the corner to the shop, but failed to return. He then searched for her and found her in Crimble Wood with another man. He accused her of 'being up to her old tricks again' and they began to argue. The two men then fought and when the other ran away, Martyn turned on Edith and strangled her.

On Monday 2 October, with Martyn on remand in prison, his father, traumatised by events and the situation his son now found himself in, collapsed and died.

Walter Martyn stood trial at Manchester Assizes on 21 November. The prosecution case was based on another version of events Martyn had told detectives following his arrest. In this account he said that they walked to the woods together where he told her he was considering leaving his job. Edith had told him if he did she would end their relationship and find another man to support her. Martyn claimed he had lost his temper, pushed her against a tree and then strangled her with a handkerchief so tightly that it left a deep groove in her neck, breaking the skin.

His defence claimed he was guilty just of manslaughter committed on provocation. On top of this they suggested that Martyn was insane and suffered morbid and depressing thoughts along with fits of uncontrollable passion.

The jury retired for over three hours and twice returned to ask trial judge Mr Justice Avory for advice on points of law, before reaching their verdict. Numerous petitions were raised in and around Heywood asking for a reprieve on a variety of grounds: the lack of premeditation, the prisoner's mental state and compassion at the recent loss of his own father. None of these swayed the Home Secretary, who announced that the execution must go ahead as planned.

42

THE GIRL OF HIS DREAMS

Arthur Birkett, 23 July 1912

Despite the terrible murder that had been committed, great effort went into trying to save the life of the prisoner awaiting execution. A petition raised over 60,000 signatures, including that of the victim's mother, and as the fateful day drew ever closer his own mother even wrote personally to the Queen begging for mercy. But it was all in vain.

In the spring of 1912, 22-year-old Arthur Birkett had been courting 18-year-old Alice Beetham for just a matter of weeks when she ended their relationship. They met while working together at the Jubilee Mill, Blackburn, and although Birkett seemed to have found the girl of his dreams, it seems that Alice wasn't quite as sure it was the great romance of her life. The relationship effectively ended when they were seen together by her father while talking and holding hands on a street corner. Believing that was no way for a courting couple to behave, he ordered Birkett to take the girl home at once. It seems that words must have been said that night at home, because a few days later Alice told Birkett she was ending their relationship. Birkett took the news badly and made a number of threats, claming that if he couldn't have Alice as his girl then no one would; to one friend he stated that he would 'chop her bloody head off!'

On Monday 20 May, as workers at the mill were taking a morning tea break, Birkett made his way to the weft shed where Alice was also on a tea break. As the hooter sounded and she made her way back to work, Birkett approached and spoke to her. Witnesses claimed that she seemed to ignore him and began to walk away. Birkett followed her – and workers looked on horrified as he grabbed her by the shoulder, put his arm round her neck and cut her throat. As blood spurted from Alice's neck, Birkett turned the razor on himself, gashing his own neck and falling to the ground at Alice's side. Both were rushed to hospital, but it was too late for Alice: she had already died from her injuries.

Birkett remained in Blackburn Infirmary, where he recovered enough to stand trial before Mr Justice Bucknill at Manchester on 5 July. The prosecution claimed that Birkett had killed the woman he loved because she had rejected him, and that when asked why he done it Birkett had said it was because he did not want anyone else but her, and as she did not want him, he could not bear the thought of her finding another man.

Birkett collapsed in the dock when sentence of death was passed on him; he walked to the gallows four days before his 23rd birthday. Outside his mother's house on Riley Street in Blackburn, a large crowd – including over 200 of his former workmates – waited for the clock to strike 8 a.m. before singing loudly 'Nearer My God to Thee'

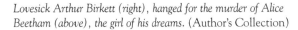
Lovesick Arthur Birkett (right), hanged for the murder of Alice Beetham (above), the girl of his dreams. (Author's Collection)

43

'L' IS FOR LIZ

James Ryder, 13 August 1913

To the jealous husband the message on the postcard was suspicious. Though the contents were bland, it began 'Dear L' and was signed 'Yours P.' Forty-seven-year-old James Ryder accused his wife Elizabeth of having an affair. Elizabeth denied anything untoward. She admitted that she was 'L' for Liz, but claimed that 'P' was simply her Aunt Polly. This did not satisfy Ryder.

Ryder lived with his wife at 32 Briscoe Street, Ardwick, Manchester, and the alcoholic sailor mistreated his wife to such an extent that she was happy only when he was away from home. They had two grown-up sons, but both had left the house, partly due to the overbearing, brutal nature of their father. By 1913, things had deteriorated to the extent that, on one of her husband's absences from home, the sons moved back home, so that they could protect their mother if called upon.

On 8 May, Ryder returned home from his latest voyage, but seeing his two sons there, he decided not to stay, only to return the following day in order to pick up some things. This time, after some discussion, he chose to stay, but the following day the arguments over the postcard began again. That night Elizabeth retired to her bed in the kitchen while her husband and sons shared the one bedroom upstairs.

On Thursday 15 May the sons rose at 5 a.m. and left for work shortly afterwards. At lunchtime the eldest returned home and discovered the body of his mother lying in the upstairs bedroom, her throat cut and with her son's own razor lying next to her.

Ryder was soon arrested and confessed to killing his wife while drunk. He said that he had been drinking in the nearby Cricketers Inn, and by closing time was so drunk that the landlord refused to serve him. He was then alleged to have confessed to the murder of his wife.

When he appeared before Mr Justice Bailache on 6 July, Ryder claimed to know nothing about the crime. The prosecution claimed that Ryder had lured his wife into the bedroom so that he could make love to her and when she resisted he cut her throat. The only motive was the anger and jealousy he had felt following the postcard he believed had been sent by a lover of his wife's.

44

THE OLDHAM COWBOYS

Ernest Edward Kelly, 17 December 1913

Fifty-four-year-old Daniel Wright Bardsley had run a profitable bookselling and stationary business on Yorkshire Street, Oldham. He employed three staff: two women, Annie Leech and Clara Hall, and 17-year-old Edward Wild Hilton, who worked as a packer and errand boy. On Saturday 26 July 1913, Bardsley told Hilton that his work was not of the required standard and he was terminating his employment.

Hilton, who had been at a school for pupils with special needs, pleaded for a second chance, promising he would 'shape up'. Bardsley said he would reconsider, but by close of his business he told the boy he was not suited to the work, and let him go.

In the early hours of the following morning the body of Bardsley was found lying face down in a pool of blood. He had been battered to death with a metal dumbbell and a wooden club.

Clara Hall told officers that earlier that previous afternoon she had gone to a local jeweller to collect half a dozen sovereign rings, so that Bardsley could chose one without having to leave the premises. She also mentioned that she was present when her boss had told the young lad Hilton that he was terminating his employment, and that the rings had been on the desk when that conversation took place.

Hilton was asked for his movements after he finished work, and, avoiding eye contact with detectives, he said he had met his friend Ernie outside the shop and that they had gone to the fair at Hollinwood. He had returned home shortly after midnight and gone straight to bed. Asked where detectives could find Ernie, Hilton claimed that he didn't know his full name or where he lived. A subsequent search of his room found bloodstained clothes, and he was arrested on suspicion of murder.

'Ernie' was found to be Ernest Edward Kelly, a 20-year-old piecer who worked at nearby Platt Brothers cotton mill. He initially denied any knowledge of the murder, but he then admitted that he had broken into the shop and struck Bardsley twice with a wooden club. However, he insisted the man was alive when he left. He handed officers a quantity of money and four sovereign rings he had taken from the office.

The two youngsters each blamed the other for the fatal blows when they stood before Mr Justice Avory at Manchester Assizes, on Monday 24 November. Hilton admitted that on the night of the murder he had been dismissed from his position at the shop. He said that he had arranged to meet Kelly after work and they planned to go to the fairground. When neither found they had any money, and Hilton said he had just been sacked, Kelly suggested that they rob the bookshop. Hilton said he wanted to wait until Bardsley had locked up and gone, but Kelly quickly rushed home to pick up a wooden club. When he returned they entered the building and attacked the shopkeeper.

Hilton said he had entered the shop and told Bardsley he forgotten his apron. As he went to collect it, he heard a cry and turned to see Kelly standing over the unconscious man and holding the bloodstained club. They went upstairs to the office to collect the rings and money and when they heard moaning and stumbling from downstairs Hilton went to help his former employer.

As he tended to the victim, Kelly had walked over, forced a handkerchief into the man's mouth and battered him about the head.

Kelly's version of events differed greatly. He said it was Hilton who suggested they carry out the robbery in revenge for having been dismissed. Kelly said that Hilton had suggested he go fetch the wooden club in case they needed a weapon to scare Bardsley into handing over the money. He said that as they waited for the women to leave work, Hilton had passed him a handkerchief, which he suggested he use to cover his face, while he did the same thing.

Kelly said that Bardsley disturbed them as they rummaged around the packing room. Hilton pulled out a replica gun and told him to 'stick-em-up'. Bardsley panicked and tried to flee, making for the back door, but he tripped and fell to the ground. Kelly then admitted he had struck the bookseller, but that was just to try to quieten him down – and as he was trying to make him comfortable, Hilton struck him several times about the head before emptying his pockets.

Summing up the case, Mr Justice Avory told the jury that it didn't matter who struck the fatal blow if both youths had been present when the fatal blows were struck, and if both had been present on a joint venture, then both were equally guilty. The jury needed just fifteen minutes to return a guilty verdict, adding a recommendation for mercy on account of their youth.

Hilton had recently turned 18 and was therefore liable to the death penalty, but it was soon announced that, as he was under that age at the time of the murder, his sentence was to be commuted to life imprisonment. This caused a great deal of outrage among the folk of Oldham, for despite the brutal savagery of the attack many believed it was Hilton who should bear the brunt of the blame, and that if anyone should have been reprieved, it should have been Kelly.

Numerous petitions were gathered, some containing many thousands of signatures, and as the date of the execution drew near Members of Parliament were lobbied and letters sent to Queen Mary, including one from Kelly's mother who described her son as 'the less guilty of the two'.

Kelly's representatives also produced evidence that the condemned man was immature, with the mental age of a 14-year-old. They showed a photograph taken just a few days before the murder in which Hilton and Kelly posed together dressed as cowboys, with Hilton holding the replica gun he had used in the robbery. It was all to no avail.

Right: *Oldham cowboys Edward Hilton and Ernie Kelly.* (Author's Collection)

Below: *Photograph of Hilton following his reprieve.* (Author's Collection)

On Tuesday evening, 16 December 1913, a telegram was sent to Kelly's family from the Home Secretary's office:

> I am sorry to be obliged to refuse to see you. I have given the fullest and most anxious consideration to the representations which have been made to me to mitigate the sentence passed on Kelly, and I deeply regret that I can come to no other decision than that which has been conveyed to you, and it must be regarded as final.
> R. McKenna
> Home Secretary

Realising that their efforts had been in vain and the law was going to take its course, an angry mob marched towards Strangeways Gaol, smashing windows as they chanted angrily and vented their wrath at the Home Secretary. Bricks where hurled through windows at Werneth police station, Oldham, and with the situation becoming critical, mounted police were summoned from surrounding districts to drive the crowds back. Several police officers were violently assaulted as they tried to break up the melee.

Having armed themselves with sticks, crowbars and a variety of shovels and spades, the angry mob reached the end of Southall Street opposite the prison gates, and a standoff commenced as dawn broke.

At 8 a.m. Kelly was hanged and later that afternoon a mourning card was produced that stated, 'In loving memory of Ernest Kelly, who was executed at Strangeways Prison, Manchester on December 17th, 1913, notwithstanding the protests of over 50,000 citizens of Oldham.'

Edward Wild Hilton was released on 9 September 1933, serving almost twenty years for his part in the murder that almost caused a riot.

The Illustrated Police News *account of the execution of Ernest Kelly.* (T.J. Leech Archive)

45

HER UNFAITHFULNESS

Frederick Holmes, 8 March 1916

In the four years since she had separated from her husband George after he discovered she had been unfaithful, 38-year-old Sarah Woodhall had taken a string of lovers and had a reputation as a prostitute. Despite her immoral reputation, Sarah was still a very attractive woman, and men liked to be seen in her company. She often drank in pubs with strangers even though she had just recently set up home with her latest man, Frederick Holmes, a 44-year-old plasterer who lived on Clifford Street, Chorlton-on-Medlock.

Sarah's mother had recently died, leaving her daughter a house in Ardwick, and with the freedom of a place of her own she was soon using the house for secret assignations. One night at the beginning of December 1915 she returned to the Ardwick house with a man she had met in a local pub. As they approached the front door they found Holmes waiting outside. There ensued a fierce argument that ended when the enraged Holmes made threats to kill her; he then walked home leaving her to spend the night in Ardwick. Sarah returned home on the following morning with her new lover.

On the morning of 8 December, Holmes left his house and went to work as usual, locking the door behind him. He did not return that evening. The following day, the landlady called round to to Clifford Street to collect the rent and, discovering no one at home, let herself in with a pass key. Finding the place in darkness she drew back the curtains, and as daylight flooded the room a gruesome sight greeted her.

On the bed lay a woman's body, slumped face down in a large pool of blood with a razor blade lying next to it. The police were called and a surgeon determined that the woman, who they had since learned was Sarah Woodhall, had died as a result of having her throat cut from ear to ear. The doctor found that she been dead for roughly thirty-six hours, and detectives learned from a friend that Sarah would have been carrying a small amount of money, which was now missing – along with the tenant of the house, Fred Holmes.

A description of Holmes was circulated throughout the area and within a short time he had been arrested, questioned and subsequently charged with murder. He told detectives that although he was guilty of murder he wanted the term 'with malice aforethought' removed from the charge sheet before he would sign the statement.

When he appeared before Mr Justice Bailhache, at Manchester Assizes on 18 February 1916, the best that the defence could offer was that Sarah had received her injuries after a struggle and that the death was an accident. It was a hopeless case, and was easily countered by the prosecution who claimed Holmes had simply killed her because she had been unfaithful to him. The jury agreed and took less than an hour to return a verdict of guilty of murder and the judge, draped with the black cap, pronounced the sentence.

46

IN A FIT OF TEMPER

Reginald Haslam, 29 March 1916

Thirty-five-year-old Isabella 'Bella' Holmes-Conway had separated from her husband shortly after the outbreak of the First World War and was living with Reg Haslam, a 25-year-old labourer, also separated from his partner, in a small house on Ellis Street, Burnley. Bella had a fondness for male company and more than once had come up with excuses for romantic nights away from home with men she had recently met up with. Bella had one lover in particular she was fond of, a young soldier called Johnny Todd, who had recently returned home after suffering from shell shock in France, and who she would invite back to her house while Haslam was at work at the engineering factory.

On 19 December 1915 Haslam told Bella that he was going to visit his mother for a few days and see his younger brother who was due to be posted overseas in the New Year. He told her that he would be back before Christmas and she walked with him to the station to catch his train. As soon as he was gone, Bella moved Todd into the house – but Haslam arrived home sooner than expected. He had forgotten to take his key and had to knock on the door to gain entry. When Bella saw him standing in the rain she told him to come back later, but he began shouting to be let in. When she eventually opened the door it was to let the young soldier make his getaway.

Haslam was known for his fiery temper, but in this case his anger was not focused on the fleeing soldier but on the woman who had been cheating on him. They had a blazing row, but eventually Bella was able to use her charm on him and he forgave her indiscretions. Things might have blown over if Bella had not started to tease him about her affair when they had a quarrel over something trivial the following day.

On 23 December, Reg Haslam walked into the local police station and confessed he had killed Bella. He told the police to visit his house where they would find the woman's body. He claimed he had strangled her in a fit of temper. Detectives hurried to the house and found that Haslam was

Burnley murderer Reg Haslam and his victim Bella Conway (right). (Author's Collection)

telling the truth: Isabella Holmes-Conway was lying dead on the front room sofa with a tightly knotted ribbon around her neck.

Haslam stood trial at the Spring Assizes at Manchester before Mr Justice Bailhache. The prosecution put forward a strong case of murder committed through jealousy and there was only a weak defence of provocation. The jury retired and returned with a verdict of guilty of murder, but with a strong recommendation for mercy.

Passing sentence of death the judge added that the recommendation for mercy would be forwarded to the appropriate office, at which Haslam cried out, 'Mercy! I don't want any mercy!'

A reprieve had already been refused when Haslam's solicitor was contacted by a member of the jury, who told him that two members of the jury had only agreed to a guilty verdict as they had believed a reprieve would be granted. A last-minute plea for clemency to the Home Secretary failed to alter the verdict, as did two petitions, one signed by soldiers in the trenches in France and the other by hundreds of local people.

47

THE LAYABOUTS

James Howarth Hargreaves, 19 December 1916

Hargreaves was 54-year-old alcoholic layabout who lodged with his sister, Savinah Hindley, at 9 Orange Street, Ashton-under-Lyne. Also living at the house was 36-year-old Caroline McGhee. Ostensibly she was also a tenant, but she and Hargreaves were having an on-off relationship which began shortly after Caroline McGhee separated from her husband in early 1914, and returned to live with her mother in Ashton. In the autumn of 1915, she met Hargreaves, and went to lodge in Orange Street. A few weeks later she moved out and went to stay with her brother, but within days she moved back in with Hargreaves on a more permanent basis.

Neither seemed willing to hold down any type of regular employment, both being layabouts who spent much of their time in the various hostelries in the area, often appearing at opening time and staying until the landlord turfed them out onto the street at closing time.

On 8 August 1916, Caroline McGhee spent the afternoon drinking with a friend, Lily Armitage, and later met up with Hargreaves in the Nelson Tavern where they stayed drinking until 6.45 p.m., at which time Hargreaves left to go home. Caroline went back to Lily's house for a short time and later they made their way to the Commercial Hotel, where they began chatting to two soldiers.

Caroline, Lily and the two soldiers, William Sumner and Edward Uttley, then collected a bottle of whiskey and went back to Hargreaves' house, and when Caroline suggested that they should have some supper Hargreaves went out to purchase some tripe. Shortly before midnight, Lily Armitage and William Sumner left together, and a short time later Uttley also departed.

Savinah Hindley had retired to bed before the guests had arrived, and the following morning she rose at dawn and found that Hargreaves was already up and about. She noticed a number of empty glasses on the table, and as her brother seemed to be rambling and mumbling that he wished he was dead, she just assumed he had been drinking late into the night and was still very drunk.

At 2.30 p.m. Hargreaves was walking along nearby Katherine Street when he spotted police constable Robert Wilson. 'Oh Bob, what shall I do, I've murdered a woman at our house!' He cried, handing over his door key.

The officer went to the house and found Caroline McGhee, lying in just her underwear, face down in a pool of blood on Hargreaves' bed. She had a large wound to the back of her head, presumably caused by the bloodstained poker that lay on the carpet.

Hargreaves appeared before Mr Justice Avory at Manchester Assizes on 28 November. He initially said he had no recollection of committing the crime, although his counsel then claimed that Mrs

Hargreaves' death certificate listed cause of death as judicial execution. (Author's Collection)

McGhee had attacked him in a drunken fury, striking him several times with her fists, and finally throwing the whisky bottle they had been sharing at him, causing him to lose control and retaliate.

The prosecution argued that it was a brutal and violent crime, and that he had killed her following a quarrel when he refused to let the soldier she had brought home stay the night. Once he had left they had finished the bottle of whiskey and when she had picked up and thrown the empty bottle at him he had grabbed the poker and struck her over the head.

With Hargreaves being just a short man, but weighing a hefty 203lbs, hangman Ellis gave him a drop of just 5ft 4in, one of the shortest drops allowed. Ellis recalled later that when he reached the gaol he discovered that he knew the condemned man and that they had often chatted at various dog-racing events. On the morning of the execution Hargreaves was too overcome with terror to recognise his executioner, and he had to be assisted to the scaffold, as he was unable to walk, such was his dread. Instead of the usual time of around ten seconds, Ellis said it took almost a minute for the terrified prisoner to reach the scaffold.

48

THE RELUCTANT SOLDIER

Thomas Clinton, 21 March 1917

Private Tommy Clinton was a reluctant soldier. The 28-year-old Mancunian had taken the King's shilling in the summer of 1916 and joined 'B' Company of the 5th Home Service Battalion Royal Welsh Fusiliers, whose barracks were near Cavendish Dock, Barrow-in Furness.

It was in the autumn of that year that he first came into contact with the fearsome Company Sergeant-Major Henry Lynch. Lynch was a professional soldier, and by the age of thirty-nine he had amassed close on 22 years service. 'B' Company was at this time on temporary manoeuvres at

Bebington, in Merseyside, when at the end of October there was some trouble in the guardroom which resulted in Clinton being placed under arrest for being drunk and disorderly.

Back at Barrow, on 4 November, Private Clinton was summoned before the company commander, Captain Webb, and after testimony by Sergeant-Major Lynch, Clinton was sentenced to seven days imprisonment and fined heavily. From that moment on he bore a grudge against Henry Lynch.

On Saturday 13 January 1917, Clinton crossed swords with Sergeant Major Lynch once again. Clinton was among a party of fourteen men on guard duty and he was due to cover the main gate between 7 p.m. and 9 p.m. He was issued with twenty rounds of ammunition, fifteen of which he kept in the pouch on his belt (the other five being loaded in his rifle).

There was a kit inspection in the early afternoon and due to this Clinton missed his lunch. It was part of his duty to stay in the guardroom when not patrolling the main gate and, disgruntled at missing his lunch, he complained to a lieutenant, who told Clinton he would sort it out. Unfortunately, the officer was called away on important business and neglected to pass on Clinton's grievance.

Later that afternoon Clinton called into the orderly room and asked Sergeant-Major Lynch if he could do something about him missing his meal. Lynch harshly dismissed Clinton's request, and brusquely told the private he was not concerned about his problem as his duties only covered matters of discipline.

Clinton returned to the guardroom in a rage, picked up his rifle, and walked back towards the orderly room. Lynch was still seated at the table tending to some paperwork; two other officers were present. Clinton approached the door, entered and lifted his rifle into the 'on-guard' position.

'Now then, Sergeant Major', Clinton said loudly, pointing the gun as he spoke. Lynch looked up at the private, and seeing the rage in his face he held up his hands. Clinton fired one shot, which hit Lynch in the neck. Dropping the weapon to the floor, Clinton walked out of the room, dropped to his knees, covered his face with his hands, and burst into tears.

Sergeant-Major Lynch staggered from his chair and followed Clinton into the corridor, but collapsed after just a few steps.

Although committed in an army barracks, the crime was in the jurisdiction of Barrow police and detectives hurried to the camp and placed Clinton under arrest. As he was taken into custody Clinton enquired about Sergeant Major Lynch.

'Will you answer me one question: did the bullet strike him? That is what I want to know. He was a scamp to everyone in the company. I am sorry to say that he is a bad 'un.'

CERTIFICATE OF SURGEON.

31 *Vic. Cap.* 24.

I, **William Norwood East** the Surgeon of His Majesty's Prison of **MANCHESTER** hereby certify that I this day examined the Body of **Thomas Clinton**, on whom Judgment of Death was this day executed in the said Prison; and that on that Examination I found that the said **Thomas Clinton** was dead.

Dated this twenty first *day of* March 1917

(Signature)

Clinton's notice of execution.
(Author's Collection)

At this time the extent of the man's injuries were not yet known, and the escort told Clinton he didn't know for certain, but thought Lynch was still alive.

Lynch died shortly after Clinton was taken into custody and in due course he found himself before Mr Justice Shearman at Manchester Assizes on 14 February 1917. His defence was that his rifle went off accidentally, but the prosecution alleged that the killing was a deliberate act carried out by a man bearing a grudge against the officer.

'There are just two verdicts open to you,' the judge told the jury prior to retirement. 'In this lamentable case there is no question of manslaughter. It is either murder or an acquittal.'

It took just twenty minutes to find Clinton guilty. Asked if he had anything to say before sentence of death was passed, Clinton said, 'Although the jury has found me guilty, there was one Judge above all present, who although we cannot see him, he knows that I am innocent'.

An appeal failed and Clinton, the reluctant soldier, met his death on the scaffold at Strangeways Gaol. He was hanged in his prison clothes, instead of his army uniform, the only other clothes he possessed, as it was considered a disgrace to the King's uniform for a man to be hanged in it.

49

HIS BROTHER'S WIFE

William Rooney, 17 December 1918

William Rooney had been too old to be conscripted as the First World War entered a decisive phase in the latter days, but he had watched proudly as his younger brother marched bravely off to France. A few weeks later, in July 1918, his brother was killed in action, leaving behind a wife and four stepchildren.

Thirty-year-old Mary Ellen Rooney had now lost two husbands and was in a vulnerable situation when her dead husband's older brother, 51-year-old William Rooney, began to make a play for her. Following her husband's death, Mary had returned to her mother's home at 17 Elm Grove, Kensington, Liverpool. William lived just a few houses away, and within days he began to call on her offering support. Initially it was well received, but Rooney soon made his intentions clear, and the young widow was not in the least receptive to his advances.

Rooney took no heed of her polite attempts to decline his advances, and when on one occasion he called round to her house drunk and she refused him entry, he threatened her with a knife. It was then she decided to relocate to the south coast and out of his way.

The move south was not a success and she decided she would not be scared away from her home. She returned to Liverpool in the early autumn. She managed to avoid Rooney for several weeks until he learned of her return. He again made attempts to start a relationship, and each time she told him she was not interested. Following the final rebuff he threatened her harm if she didn't change her mind.

To compound matters Mary's mother had taken in a lodger while her daughter was away and when she returned to the house she found the young soldier pleasant company and accepted his invitation to go out for a drink.

When Rooney discovered that the soldier had taken Mary out he made threats against them. When he saw them out shopping on Saturday 2 November 1918 it was the final straw: he followed her into a shop and stabbed her through the neck.

At his Manchester trial on 25 November before Mr Justice Lush, Rooney offered a plea of insanity. His counsel claimed Rooney's father, two brothers and a sister had all been in an asylum, which showed a strong family history of insanity. They also testified that Rooney claimed to have seen his dead brother's spirit on a number of occasions, but the jury were not convinced by Rooney's defence and he was convicted of wilful murder (see previous story).

50

ON THE FACTORY FLOOR

Hyman Perdovitch, 6 January 1920

Hyman Perdovitch had suffered greatly fighting for the Allies in the First World War. Born in Vilna, Russia, in 1880, he had moved to England as a young man and when war was declared he was happy to risk his life for his adopted country. He enlisted in 1916 and while serving in the Royal Irish Regiment he fought at Ypres. In one fierce conflict with the Kaiser's army he was so badly injured that he lost the lower part of his left leg.

As a result, he was invalided out of the army, and on his return to Salford, once he recovered sufficiently, he returned to his job at Messrs Wilks Bros., a Salford-based waterproofing manufacturers, working in the small factory with many other returning soldiers and a number of apprentices. Perdovitch's disability necessitated regular visits to Salford Royal Hospital for treatment to his wound, and this resulted in long periods of absence from work.

The foreman at the factory was 48-year-old Soloman Franks, the head of a large family from Cheetham Hill, Manchester, and although both Franks and Perdovitch were members of the same Jewish faith they did not get on well together. Perdovitch often complained to his workmates that the foreman treated him like a dog, gave him all the dirty jobs, and claimed that Franks resented him taking time off work to visit hospital. For several months Perdovitch let this anger with his boss smoulder – until he finally exploded.

On the morning of Friday 15 August 1919, Perdovitch left his home in Sedgley Park, Prestwich, and made his way to work, clocking on at the factory as normal. After chatting to a colleague over a cup of tea he went to his bench and began the day's work. A few minutes later Franks walked into the shop. They didn't speak as the foreman passed his machine, but as he headed towards the door Perdovitch picked up a pocket knife, rushed up to Franks and plunged it twice into the back of his neck. A shocked workmate cried out, 'Hymie, what have you done?'

Perdovitch replied calmly, 'You can see what I've done, I am the injured man. You know how he treated me. I have done it and now I am waiting for the police like a man'.

With that he turned and walked out of the factory. At two minutes to nine that morning Perdovitch calmly strolled into Salford police station and asked the desk sergeant, 'Do you want me?'

Asked why he should be wanted, he replied, 'That affair at Wilks'. If you don't want me now you soon will!'

He then confessed he had stabbed his foreman and when police hurried to the factory they found Soloman Franks bleeding profusely from two wounds in his neck. A workmate had administered first aid, but the foreman was clearly in need of proper medical care. He was rushed to Salford Royal Hospital, where he died soon after admittance. Perdovitch, already in custody following his initial confession, was then charged with murder.

He stood trial at Manchester Assizes on Friday 5 December, before Mr Justice McCardie. The prosecution alleged that Perdovitch had brutally stabbed Franks to death in a cold premeditated act, as the result of a grudge he believed the foreman bore against him. In his defence, Perdovitch claimed he hadn't intended to commit murder and had only struck out at Franks with the intention of hurting him.

It was no real defence against a murder charge, and after a short hearing the jury retired for just twenty minutes before they returned a guilty verdict, with a strong recommendation for mercy. On 6 January 1920 Hyman Perdovitch gained the dubious distinction of being the first Jew to be executed at Strangeways prison.

51

REVENGE

David Caplan, 6 January 1920

When Freda Waterman met her husband-to-be, Polish-born David Caplan, in the summer of 1910 it was love at first sight; nine years and two children later and, although still together, the happy path of married bliss had long since eroded away. She had, mainly for the children's sake, been forced to endure long periods of unhappiness, mostly due to his frequent outbursts of violence.

In 1917 the Caplan family were living with Freda's mother in Liverpool while preparations where made to secure a house in Leeds. Once the house had been acquired they set off across the Pennines, but it was not long before Freda and the children were back in the bosom of her own family.

She told her mother that her husband was ill-treating her and was invited to stay as long as she liked. A few days later David Caplan came to the house and, promising to mend his ways, escorted his family back to Yorkshire. During the next two years Freda and the children made the journey back to Liverpool ten times, and each time her husband came in hot pursuit, full of apologies and assurances that it wouldn't happen again.

In the summer of 1919, the whole family finally packed up and moved back to Liverpool, once again settling at Mrs Waterman's. Three weeks later they moved into their own home, a flat above a shop on Derby Road, Kirkdale.

Caplan, a 42-year-old ex-sailor, managed to find a job in a local engineering works, while his wife ran a millinery business in the shop downstairs. During a fierce quarrel in August Caplan struck his wife. In tears Freda told him that she would inform the police if he didn't leave her alone, to which he coldly retorted, 'If you go to the police I will kill you and burn down the shop.'

On 9 September Freda's sister Minnie, who looked after the children while Freda ran the shop, entered the flat and found broken dinner plates on the floor. Caplan told her that he had thrown the plates at Freda because he lost his temper after she kept asking him for money.

On 13 October Freda Caplan took out a summons for assault against her husband, resulting in a brief appearance in court and a 10s fine. Caplan told his wife after the court case that he would get his revenge on her.

'You will swing for it if you do,' she mocked.

'I don't care,' he replied calmly.

The next day a neighbour heard loud screams, at intervals, coming from the shop, followed by a low moaning which she thought might be Mrs Caplan. The police were called and on gaining entry found the bodies of Freda Caplan and her two children in a bedroom. They had been beaten to death with a bloodstained flat iron, which lay at the foot of the bed. Caplan was found lying on the floor of the shop downstairs with a self-inflicted throat wound made by a razor, recovered in the kitchen. He was taken to hospital, where it was soon discovered that his wounds were only superficial. He was then charged with the murder of his wife and children.

Although the crime had been committed in Liverpool he was summoned to appear at the Manchester Assizes. He stood before Mr Justice Macardie on Tuesday 2 December 1919. The prosecution alleged that it was a cold-blooded, premeditated murder while the defence could only offer a plea of insanity on the grounds that Caplan was not responsible for his actions, adding that the defendant maintained he had no recollection of the killings.

As two men had been sentenced to death at the same assizes, it was decided that they would hang together, a rare event at Manchester, and on a cold January morning Caplan was led to the scaffold and hanged along side Hyman Perdovitch, the Russian Jew who had murdered his foreman in Salford.

52

UNCONTROLLABLE PASSION

Frederick Rothwell Holt, 13 April 1920

On the morning of Christmas Eve 1919, a farmer out on a morning stroll noticed footsteps in the wet sand leading towards the sand hills at St Anne's. Following them, he came across the body of 28-year-old Kathleen 'Kitty' Harriet Breaks. She had been shot dead. Lying next to the body was a bloodstained man's glove and the woman's handbag.

The handbag contained money and papers, which seemed to rule out the motive of robbery, and apart from the money there was a collection of love letters, all signed 'Eric'.

Eric turned out to be Frederick Rothwell Holt, a former soldier living in Blackpool. A search of the beach soon uncovered a revolver buried in a shallow grave in a nearby sand hill. The serial number had been erased from the cylinder, but a series of numbers stamped on the hand strap had been overlooked. This was traced to a Preston gunsmith who told detectives he had sold the gun to Holt in 1914. Holt was arrested the following morning.

Holt had been called up as an officer in the Territorial Army at the outbreak of the First World War in 1914. After taking part in some of the bloodiest battles in France he was invalided out, suffering from shell shock and rheumatism.

Holt had met Kitty Breaks at Middlesborough when she was living apart from her husband. They soon fell in love and with her now living in Bradford he made frequent trips to spend weekends with her. In May 1919 Holt had approached the Atlas Insurance Co. to enquire about taking out an insurance policy on Kitty for £10,000. His request was refused, mainly because, as he was not married to her, he could have no claim on her estate if she was to die.

Two months before her death, on 14 October, Holt successfully insured Kitty for £5,000, but unsuccessfully tried to take out a further two policies for £10,000 each. Holt had also persuaded her to make her will in his favour, which she signed on 17 December.

Eric Holt (left) and Kitty Breaks.
(Both Author's Collection)

On 22 December Holt travelled to Bradford and spent the night with Kitty at her lodgings and the following day she took possession of the insurance policy and they travelled back together to Blackpool. She arranged to meet Holt later that night at St Anne's. The following morning she was shot dead

Frederick Holt stood before Mr Justice Greer in February 1920 at Manchester Assizes. Although his fate looked grim he had arguably one of the best defence counsels of his time, Sir Edward Marshall Hall, in his corner. Marshall Hall tried to contend that Holt was mentally unfit to stand trial, but this was rejected. Holt's defence was based around the issue of insanity, but after a five-day trial it took less than an hour for the jury to find him guilty as charged.

Asked if he had anything to say before sentence of death was passed, he shrugged his shoulders and looked at the clock. Sentenced to death, he glanced quickly around the court and told the guard as he left the dock, 'Well, that's over. I hope my tea won't be late!'

Marshall was convinced that Holt was mad and made strenuous efforts to get the verdict overturned. It was in vain. Prior to the execution Marshall Hall wrote to Holt's solicitors:

> I feel so strongly that he is now mad, and, as a man, contemplate with horror the idea of executing a madman, that I am willing you should, if you think fit, to communicate the contents of this letter to the Home Secretary or to the Attorney General. As you know I have never had any doubts in my own mind that Holt's hand fired the shot that killed Mrs Breaks, nor have I ever had any real doubt that the deed was done under the influence of some uncontrollable passion acting on a mind enfeebled by shell shock and disease.

Holt remained callous to the end, indifferent to the campaigns for a reprieve that his family were orchestrating outside the prison walls. Hangman John Ellis watched Holt at exercise on the afternoon before the execution and noted that he was a fine, strapping six-footer who looked like an athlete in training as he strode around the exercise yard with the warder puffing in his wake.

During discussion with prison officers, Ellis asked if they believed Holt really was insane. 'He's not mad at all,' he was told, 'all he has done since he came into the condemned cell is complain. We'll all be glad when it's over and he is gone!'

At 8 a.m. the following morning the hangmen entered the cell. Holt was standing facing the door with a cigarette dangling between his lips as they approached to pinion his arms. Holt glared at them. 'Is this really necessary?' Ellis replied it was as he strapped Holt's arms behind his back. Holt repeated the question to the Chief Warder standing across the table and, when told it was, he clenched his fist as if to try to pull free. Holt walked slowly towards the scaffold then stopped a few feet short of the drop. He glared at Ellis and refused to move. Willis gave him a timely push and they managed to get him under the beam. As Ellis went to place the cotton bag over his head Holt again complained, 'you're not going to put that on!' 'Oh yes I must,' Ellis replied, standing on his tiptoes to reach. Ellis said that the last look from Holt was one of sheer hatred. Seconds later, with the noose secured, he darted to the lever and the trapdoors crashed open.

53

THE CLIFTON CUT-THROAT MURDER

William Thomas Aldred, 22 June 1920

It was a cold Monday morning, 16 February 1920, as several coal miners set off wearily up Manchester Road, Clifton, to catch the trolley bus that would take them home after a hard night's shift.

As they waited for the bus to arrive, some read the morning papers while others stood chatting, until they were interrupted by a blood-curdling scream coming from the house directly opposite the bus stop. At that same moment a young girl dashed out into the street, tears streaming down her face, yelling, 'Murder! Come quickly!'

Several of the men hurried across the road and entered the house at 90 Manchester Road where, reaching the back kitchen, they found the body of a middle-aged woman lying on the floor bleeding from a fearsome wound to her throat. Standing over her, as if in a trance, was a man holding a blood-splattered razor.

'What have you done?' Someone yelled, but the man stood motionless and shaking until a passing policeman entered the house, disarmed him and shepherded the workmen out of the room. Efforts were made to revive the stricken woman, but to no avail, and detectives based in Salford were soon at the house. The victim was identified as Ida Prescott, a 44-year-old widow, and while her body was removed to a nearby mortuary, the killer was taken into custody.

He gave his name as Bill Aldred, a 54-year-old mill worker who lived at Pendlebury. The dead woman's daughter told detectives that her mother had been friendly with Aldred for a couple of years and he had been a frequent visitor to their house. Both Aldred and Mrs Prescott were employed in a nearby mill, and police learned that Aldred had tried on many occasions to make the relationship a romantic one although Mrs Prescott seemed content to remain as just friends.

On that fateful morning Ida Prescott had taken the day off work, and shortly before 10 a.m. Aldred had called on her. Her daughter said that Aldred had asked her mother to go for a walk with him but she refused. Ida had then picked up the dirty breakfast dishes and entered the kitchen – and Aldred had followed her. She then heard them arguing, and moments later she heard a fearful moan, and turned to see her mother stagger from the kitchen clasping her throat, before slumping to the floor.

Aldred appeared before Mr Justice McCardie at Manchester Assizes on 13 May. He pleaded not guilty and his counsel claimed he was insane, supporting this with evidence that he had spent long periods in a mental hospital.

The prosecution claimed Aldred had killed Ida Prescott after she made it clear she did not want to become romantically involved with him. They said that Aldred had threatened, 'Well if I can't have you, no one can' moments before striking the fatal blow. The short trial ended with the prisoner being sentenced to death, and after an appeal failed, he was hanged on a warm summer morning.

54

THE HALLOWEEN MURDERER

Charles Colclough, 31 December 1920

New Year's Eve, Friday 31 December 1920, and despite the heavy rain, a fair-sized crowd waited in the street outside Manchester's Strangeways Gaol, as the clock ticked slowly towards 8 a.m. Behind the high, grim prison walls the last minutes in the life of Charlie Colclough, dubbed in the press as Hanley's 'Halloween Murderer', were about to be played out. At the appointed hour the hangmen would enter the cell, the condemned man would walk, or in some cases be carried, the few short steps to the gallows and, once the noose was in place, the trapdoor would open and the prisoner drop to his death.

Today's crowd was a mixture of curious locals joined by a number of spectators from Hanley, Staffordshire, the hometown of both the killer and his victim. Alongside those there paying respects to Colclough were a number who made a regular pilgrimage to the prison gates, come rain or shine, hoping to catch a glimpse of the hangman and his assistant or perhaps to hear the trapdoor crash. Colclough was the fifth man hanged at Manchester that year, giving the locals so inclined ample opportunity to quench their macabre thirst.

DRAMATIC INCIDENT
AT EXECUTION.

EXPRESS LETTER FOR DOOMED MAN

JUST TOO LATE.

COLCLOUGH PAYS PENALTY AT STRANGEWAYS TO-DAY.

Newspaper account relating
to Charles Colclough (above)
– hanged on New Year's Eve
1920. (T.J. Leech Archive)

As the minutes ticked away towards the fateful hour, the prison bell began its mournful toll. At 8 a.m. the crowd stood in silence, hats removed in honour of the man who was now dead. A warder walked from the wicket in the gate and pinned up a notice to signify the execution had been carried out, and with many of the crowd now satisfied justice had been done, a few dispersed and walked away.

It was as the bell tolled that a postman turned into Southall Street and approached the prison. He pulled out a bundle of letters as he approached the gate and the remaining crowd.

'Who are they tolling the bell for?' The postman asked one man sheltering under an umbrella.

'A man named Colclough', he was told.

'Colclough?' The postman said, shaking his head, 'I've a letter for him.' He looked at the envelope and saw it was an express letter from Whitehall.

'Hard luck, Colclough', the postman offered, posting the letters through the prison mailbox. (Although the contents of the letter were never made public it was rumoured to be a reprieve that arrived too late to save him.)

Forty-five-year-old Colclough found himself occupying the condemned cell at Strangeways for a love-affair murder. Colclough was a Hanley fish salesman, and although he was a married man, he was separated and had been living with Annie Shenton, also married but separated, since July 1920. It seemed to Colclough that they lived happily enough until, on Saturday 30 October, Annie suddenly returned to her husband, George Shenton, leaving behind a letter addressed to Colclough asking his forgiveness and warning him not to turn to drink.

The following morning, Colclough went around to Shenton's house at 15 Durham Street, Hanley. He tried the door and when it opened he entered and shouted for Shenton to come downstairs. Annie and her husband were still in bed, but she dressed and came down. Colclough repeated his call for Shenton to come down and face him – so he too dressed and followed his wife down the stairs.

According to Annie, Colclough rushed at her husband and as the two men struggled on the floor Colclough drew out a razor and dragged it, with some force, across George's throat, twice.

At his trial before Mr Commissioner Young KC at Stafford Assizes on 20 November, Colclough gave a different version of events. He claimed he had gone to the house to retrieve the £2 10s he had given to Annie for housekeeping. After entering the house, Annie appeared at the top of the stairs, and as he asked her to return the money Shenton came haring down the stairs brandishing a razor. They began to fight and, as Shenton was getting the upper hand, Colclough said he reached into his pocket to get a key he planned to use as a weapon – but instead he found himself clutching a razor he had forgotten he was carrying. Fearing for his life, he opened the razor and cut Shenton's throat. 'It was him or me,' he told the court.

The jury chose to believe the prosecution's account – that Colclough, a lover spurned, had committed a brutal, deliberate and premeditated murder – and two months to the day later he walked to the gallows as the postman made his way towards the prison gates.

55

IRRESISTIBLE IMPULSE

Frederick Quarmby, 5 April 1921

Christina Ann Smith was 31-years-old and pregnant when she married her husband in February 1913, and, later that same day, she confided to him some of the dark secrets from her past. Whatever it was she said behind the locked hotel door had an instant effect on the marriage, for by morning John Smith had packed his bags and walked out of her life for good. Following the birth of her daughter she moved alone into the house on Ripon Road, Blackpool, paid for by her estranged husband, and when Smith told her he was petitioning for a divorce she mockingly told him he could take his pick of men to cite as co-respondent.

Mrs Smith first met Fred Quarmby, an unmarried, well-educated Yorkshireman, shortly after the Armistice. He soon moved into the house on Ripon Road and they instantly began a tempestuous relationship, which often resulted in one or the other of them sporting a bruise or a black eye. They seemed to argue about almost everything, but mostly because she had what he called 'a roving eye' and always seemed to be flirting with other men.

In the autumn of 1920 they argued when he accused her of having an affair with another man. Quarmby moved out of the house on Ripon Road and took lodgings nearby, where he was soon telling fellow tenants that he was 'going to do her in'.

On the night of 3 December, Christina and Quarmby spent the night in a number of town-centre pubs before returning to Ripon Road. She invited him into the dining room and they began to quarrel over the other man. They seemed to have made up and after kissing and cuddling on the sofa they began to make love – when suddenly, he pulled out a knife and stabbed her. Her screams awoke both her 6-year-old daughter and the lodger, who began banging on the door asking if she was all right.

Quarmby continued to stab her, slashing her across the throat with such force that he almost severed her head. He then went to the back door and told the neighbour what he had done; afterwards he waited patiently for the police to arrive and take him into custody.

The trial of 47-year-old Frederick Quarmby was held at Manchester Assizes on 5 February 1921. The prosecution presented a clear-cut case of wilful murder, with the motive being jealousy. The defence offered the theory that Quarmby had committed the crime due to 'irresistible impulse', a form of insanity, and called in a specialist in mental disorders, who had examined Quarmby under hypnosis.

Mr Justice Acton, in his summing up, said that there had to be other proof that Quarmby was insane, as 'irresistible impulse' alone had never been accepted as a defence. The jury, which comprised of nine men and three women, took just fifteen minutes to find him guilty.

An appeal was held on 21 March and more evidence was permitted to try and prove Quarmby's insanity. A witness was called who had heard Quarmby threaten Christina Smith by saying, 'there will be another Holt case' (referring to the local man hanged in the previous year).

There were a series of striking parallels with the Holt case. Both men had been bachelors named Fred who had killed women living apart from their husbands; both victims were natives of Bradford, both men had worked in Nottingham, both had pleaded insanity, and both were hanged at Manchester by John Ellis.

56

'THROUGH DRINK AND OTHERS'

Thomas Wilson, 24 May 1921

Whenever Tommy Wilson's ship pulled into his homeport of Liverpool he took lodgings with 44-year-old mother of three Olive Jackson, who lived on Newby Street in Walton, Liverpool. Wilson, a year younger, had been friendly with Olive for several years, and during his stays at the house between voyages, they had often been on intimate terms. In recent years, though, she had begun a relationship with a man named George Duff, and in due course he began to live at the house on Newby Street.

While on leave during Christmas 1920, Wilson was invited to a party where one of the guests pulled out some mistletoe, and soon some of the guests were taking their chance to snatch Christmas kisses. Wilson noticed, however, that when one of the revellers, a man named Harry Roskell, went to embrace Olive it seemed a little more than a festive gesture, but when he questioned her about it later she just laughed it off.

On his next leave, in April 1921, he was again invited to a party. When he learned that Roskell would be there Wilson declined, and was saddened when later that evening Olive told him she and Duff intended to go without him. Later that evening Wilson turned up at the party and, with Duff inside and very drunk, Olive accepted his invitation to walk her home.

Olive knew that Wilson suspected that her relationship with Duff was no longer going well, and that he sensed his chance if they broke up. But she also knew Wilson was jealous and had a violent temper and as they walked home an argument began that evolved into a fierce war of words. As they returned home she turned on him and shouted, 'If anything does happen tonight, I still won't ever marry a worm like you!'

'Fair enough,' snarled Wilson, 'I'll move out tomorrow.'

'You can go tonight,' she spat back, storming out of the house and slamming the door behind her.

Wilson then picked up his gun and left the house searching for Olive Jackson. He soon spied her making her way home. He watched her from his vantage point in the shadows and as she approached he sprang out: after a brief exchange of words he fired five times, killing her instantly. A neighbour summoned the police and he was soon in police custody. When charged with the murder Wilson sobbed, 'My God, I'm sorry. It is all through drink and others!'

He made a brief appearance at Liverpool police court on 13 April and was remanded to a higher court. George Duff watched as Wilson made his way to the witness box and when he took his position between two burly guards, Duff turned and shouted, 'You murderer! You bloody murderer!' He attempted to attack the prisoner before being restrained and ushered away from the dock.

Wilson could offer no realistic defence at his trial at Manchester before Mr Justice Acton on 2 May. The prosecution claimed the crime was a result of jealousy and the confession he made following his arrest all helped to secure his guilt.

Thomas Wilson. (T.J. Leech Archive)

57

NOT WORTH AN APPEAL

Hiram Thompson, 30 May 1922

Fifty-two-year-old labourer Hiram Thompson was so resigned to his fate that he accepted the death sentence philosophically and when asked if he planned to appeal he simply replied, 'It's not worth an appeal.' Thompson had been sentenced to death by Mr Justice Branson at Manchester Assizes on 8 May 1922 for the brutal murder of his wife Ellen at their home on Brandiforth Street, Bamber Bridge, Preston.

Thompson shared his home with his wife, two sons, two daughters and a son-in-law. Theirs was not a happy home, mainly on account of Thompson's heavy drinking and the amount of money he squandered on alcohol in the local pubs. Many of these drunken quarrels would end in violence against his long-suffering wife, and as Thompson spent most nights out drinking, the quarrels and assaults became an almost daily occurrence.

On Tuesday morning on 25 April, the family rose and prepared for work and school, and by 9 a.m. Thompson and his wife remained alone in the house. They soon began to quarrel over the usual topics, but when her daughter came home for her lunch all seemed well, although Ellen told her daughter that her father had just left to go to the pub.

When the eldest daughter returned home later that afternoon she discovered the body of her mother lying in the kitchen. There was no sign of her father. Detectives traced his movements that afternoon, and found he had spent the day drinking in a number of public houses before calling on a friend to whom he confessed he had killed his wife.

Taken into custody, Thompson's clothing was found to be heavily bloodstained. In his defence he claimed that his wife had tried to attack him with the heavy flat iron she was using to press clothes and that he had disarmed her and struck a fatal blow, before cutting her throat. Forensic examination told a different story and suggested that Ellen's throat had been cut while she was standing, presumably at the ironing board, and blood had spurted all over the room.

The trial was short and lasted just a matter of hours before the jury found Thompson guilty as charged. They found no reason to recommend mercy. Hangman John Ellis later recorded that on arrival at the prison he got into conversation with a warder who had been a friend of both Thompson and his wife. Ellis said the warder was quite affected by seeing his friend in these circumstances, but Thompson had shown no signs of nerves or fear. 'He doesn't seem in the least bit bothered,' he told Ellis.

Such was Thompson's obliviousness to his fate he had to be roused from his sleep on the morning of his execution – he complained to the guards that they should have woken him earlier for his last morning on earth, but that he had slept better in prison that he ever did at home!

58

'I WILL SEE YOU OUT FIRST!'

George Frederick Edisbury, 3 January 1923

On Saturday 29 July 1922 44-year-old painter George Edisbury returned to his lodgings at 64 Higher Cambridge Street, Chorlton-on-Medlock, after a night of heavy drinking in a number of local pubs. He had not been home long when he began to argue with 50-year-old Mrs Winifred Drinkwater. It was a recurring quarrel that seemed to surface on a weekly basis.

Winifred Drinkwater and her husband, Peter, occupied two rooms in the house, which was tenanted by her brother John Oakes, an infirm, elderly man who lived mainly in the back kitchen. Winifred acted as housekeeper and landlady while Edisbury rented the middle bedroom, which he shared with Annie Grimshaw, a married woman separated from her husband with whom he had been living since 1916.

Both Edisbury and Annie were heavy drinkers, and Winifred Drinkwater was not afraid to let them know she did not approve of their lifestyle, especially as she believed that Annie often worked a prostitute and that Edisbury was living off her earnings. She also suspected that the couple were claiming a married couple's pension, which they were not entitled to.

Edisbury, now very much the worse for drink, began to remonstrate again with Winifred following derogatory remarks she had made to him that afternoon.

'My wife is not a prostitute. I am telling you that. You have wanted me out for some time, but I am telling you I will see you out first!' He shouted – before pulling out his razor and slashing Winifred across the throat. As she sank to the floor, mortally wounded, Winifred's husband returned home, and as he held her in his arms she died from her wounds.

Realising what he had done Edisbury fled the house, and after calling to see his brother in Moss Side he walked to his sister's house in Rusholme. He told her what has happened, but was so drunk his sister didn't believe what he was saying. She let him sleep on the sofa and it was there that police tracked him down the following morning.

At his Manchester Assizes trial, before Mr Justice Acton on 27 November, Edisbury said that he had no memory of the murder. He claimed that he and the dead woman were on good terms and he also said that he had no recollection of telling his sister that he had cut Winifred's throat. His counsel offered a defence of manslaughter, claiming there was no premeditation and that he had been too drunk to form any intent. The defence was rejected.

SHE DIED IN MY ARMS!

Husband Too Late to Avert Tragedy.

"I found my wife lying on the pavement, bleeding from a wound in the throat. . . . I raised her head. . . . She just moved and died in my arms." A middle-aged man was telling the Manchester Coroner the story of the tragedy he was too late to avert. He was Peter Drinkwater, the dead woman was his wife, Winifred (50), and in connection with her death George Frederick Edisbury (52) had been charged with wilful murder, and was present at the inquest.

The husband said he and his wife occupied rooms at 64 Higher Cambridge-street, Hulme, and three or four months ago Edisbury and a woman came to live at the house. Two days before the tragedy his wife told him Edisbury had insulted her and

Edisbury.

News cutting relating to the murder of Winifred Drinkwater. (T.J. Leech Archive)

59

A HANGING BEFORE
8 O'CLOCK

George Perry, 28 March 1923

Edwin and Emma Perry lived on Spencer Street, Burslem, and for the last six months Edwin's brother, George Perry, an out-of-work bicycle maker, had lodged at the house. On Boxing Day 1922, Edwin and Emma were drinking with friends in the Staff of Life public house at lunchtime; when they returned home they found 50-year-old George in a drunken state.

Later that evening Edwin Perry went upstairs to sleep, leaving his brother and wife in the kitchen. At 4.30 p.m. he rose and made his way downstairs, where he noticed his wife was asleep in the armchair. He filled the kettle, and as he went to rouse his wife he noticed that she was sitting in a pool of blood: her throat had been cut. George Perry was gone, and after summoning help from a neighbour who tried to stem the blood flow, the police were called.

As an ambulance made its way to Spencer Street, George Morris, a boatman with the Mersey Weaver Co., was sitting in his boat, *Ribble*, in the wharf at Middleport when he heard a large splash. He went to investigate and discovered George Perry floating in the water. Perry was dragged out and taken to Morris's brother's house, which was nearby. He was clearly drunk and rambling about how he was a good swimmer and should have tied a brick around his neck.

Police interviewed Perry and he soon admitted that he had cut Emma's throat: 'She has been on at me all week. I did not know what I had done until it was done.'

Perry's defence at Stafford Assizes, before Mr Justice Shearman on 22 February 1923, was that he was unaware of his actions because he was so drunk. He claimed that he had been having a relationship with his sister-in-law, although his brother strongly refuted these claims. Perry's niece, the dead woman's daughter, testified that on the morning of the murder George Perry had claimed that he would be dead soon, and that one morning in the future 'there would be a hanging before 8 o'clock'.

The defence claimed that this showed he was insane, and made reference to his family history. Realising the insanity defence was weak they also focused on offering a plea of manslaughter, but it was to no avail: Perry's prediction that there would be a hanging before 8 o'clock came true a month later.

George Perry was the second of two men sentenced to death by Mr Justice Shearman (right) to go to the gallows at Manchester. (Author's Collection)

60

THE PUNISHER

Francis Wilson Booker, 8 April 1924

On the morning of Tuesday 4 September 1923, 14-year-old Percy Sharpe left home for the first of his twice-weekly visits to the Juvenile Labour Exchange. Percy lived with his family on South Street, Ardwick, and with his father recently having to give up work with rheumatic fever, Percy, the eldest of four children, saw himself as the family breadwinner – and he was desperate to find work. Joining the queue, Percy got into a conversation with an older man who was loitering in the building. The man told him he knew where there was some work going, and if he would meet him on Oxford Road later that morning, he would help Percy find work.

At 2.30 that afternoon, from his hut, a signalman at Northenden Junction saw a young boy emerge from the adjacent wood – naked from the waist down and bleeding from a horrific chest wound. Along with a platelayer working on the line, they hurried to offer assistance.

'A man has stabbed me,' the boy moaned, pointing towards the woods. He was taken to a nearby school, where he related how he had met his unknown assailant from the labour exchange on Oxford Road. They had taken a tram to Alexander Park, Whalley Range, alighting at the Palatine Road terminus. They then took a bus to Northenden. He said the man had bought him a ginger beer before he took him into the woods – where he stabbed him in the chest after he resisted his attempts to assault him. Asked to identify his attacker, he said he was clean-shaven, wore a checked cap and mackintosh, and was middle-aged.

Percy was rushed to hospital where it was discovered he had been stabbed in the abdomen, the wound piercing the stomach wall, damaging the liver and causing massive internal bleeding. He survived an operation, but tragically his condition worsened and, with his parents sitting at his bedside, Percy Sharpe died from his injuries at 5 a.m. the following morning.

The following day a young boy playing out in Chorlton found a knife believed to be the murder weapon, but it was to be four months to the day before police got their man. In the meantime two suspects were in the frame, including a Stockport man who was arrested on suspicion before evidence was produced to clear him.

Early in the New Year, reports reached detectives that a man had been terrorising young boys in Alexander Park, Whalley Range. Several parents had complained that the man had taken it upon himself to inflict punishments on young boys who he had caught cycling or smoking in the parks: he was alleged to have struck the children with his belt or clipped them around the ear with his hand.

On 4 January 1924, a constable was sent to investigate and spotted a man chasing a group of young boys away from the park. The officer caught up with the man, who gave his name as Francis Wilson Booker, a 28-year-old unemployed warehouseman. The address he gave was a lodging house on nearby Carter Street.

Booker, with a crop of grey hair, looked much older than his 28 years. He was taken to a nearby police station and asked to empty his pockets. Inside were five notebooks chronicling punishments and beatings the self-styled 'punisher' had handed out to youngsters in the previous months. Booker was identified by several of the children whose parents had complained to the police, and as a result he was held on four counts of assault, which he admitted to.

Officers searched Booker's room at the lodging house, where they found a suitcase which contained three pairs of boy's trousers along with a diary and labour card, both of which bore the name Percy Sharpe. In an allotment on Princess Road, next to the park where he had carried out his assaults, police found a pair of bloodstained braces which, along with the torn trousers, were shown to Percy's parents. Mrs Sharpe broke down in tears as she pointed out the stitching she had done whilst repairing the trousers.

Booker repeatedly denied any involvement in the murder, but when diary, labour card and braces were placed on the table before him, he began to shake and claimed he had found them in a parcel. Asked why he hadn't reported it to the police, Booker claimed he was scared that he would fall under suspicion if he had done so.

Booker appeared before Mr Justice Greer at Manchester Assizes in February. The evidence against him was based mainly on the items found in his possession, and on the second day he was called into the dock. He hurried forward and picked up the Bible to take the oath – which he began kissing fervently. He claimed he had discovered items belonging to Percy Sharpe while cycling close to Carr's Wood. Booker said that he found the package in the road and took it home without opening it. He had forgotten about the bundle until nearly two months later when he came across it while tidying up. He claimed he couldn't remember hiding it in the cellar.

Mr Kenneth Burke, KC, Booker's counsel, told the jury in closing the defence that they should acquit the prisoner, as in his mind it was clear there was no actual evidence that Booker had committed the murder. He pointed to the evidence of witnesses who had identified another suspect as the man seen with Percy on that fateful day.

'Surely, if my client was guilty, he would have burned the incriminating evidence rather than leave it lying around where it could easily be found,' Burke asked as he concluded his defence.

The jury took just twenty-five minutes to find Booker guilty as charged, and once sentence had been passed on him Booker walked nonchalantly from the dock. An appeal was dismissed when the panel found that Booker had seemingly made a career out of corrupting little boys and was a character of the worst kind.

Following the resignation of long-standing hangman John Ellis, William Willis was selected to carry out the execution; by coincidence, Willis lived less than a mile away from the condemned man. Booker received just one visitor while in the condemned cell: his elderly father, who travelled up from Booker's hometown of Horncastle, Lincolnshire. With tears in his eyes, the old man asked how his only son, with medals for bravery awarded during the First World War, could have changed into a perverted killer.

61

THE BOY NAMED 'COPPER'

John Charles Horner, 13 August 1924

One bleak December morning in 1923, the heavy gates of Strangeways prison slammed shut behind John Charles Horner with the warning ringing in his ears to 'get on the right path before it was too late'. Horner was a 23-year-old petty criminal who had just finished a six-month stretch for theft and on his release he returned to his family and fiancée, a pretty nurse who worked at the nearby hospital, and found a job labouring at a local mill. Unfortunately, the break up of his engagement shortly before Easter set into action a chain of events that horrified the community of Pendleton.

On Tuesday 10 June 1924, 6-year-old Norman Pinchin, known to his family as 'Copper' due to his mop of bright red hair, asked his father if he could have a penny. Harold Pinchin told his youngest son that he could have a halfpenny if he promised to help around the house at the weekend, and thanking his father he hurried into the backyard where his friend 8-year-old Eric Wilson waited.

After making for the local sweet shop they then headed across the street to Peel Park, a small piece of woodland that stood between the LMS Railway line and the River Irwell at Salford, where shortly after 3 p.m. they were approached by an older man who offered to buy them both an ice cream and to show them something he had found in the canal. The lure of ice cream tempted them and they each took hold of the man's hand as he walked towards the park gate. Eric was told to go and buy the ices and given some money, but when he returned the others had vanished.

Norman had accompanied the man down the path adjacent to a canal, where a neighbour who knew Norman well saw them. He watched them walk along the path until they reached Windsor Bridge and he lost sight of them. A timber-yard labourer also witnessed events unfolding: he saw the man and young boy pass under the road bridge and out of view, but such was his curiosity that he continued to watch, expecting them to emerge from the other side. After what seemed like an age the boy emerged from under the bridge half dressed and obviously in great distress. He watched in horror as the man then picked the boy up by the scruff of the neck, hoisted him off his feet and hurled him into the dark, murky canal.

By the time the labourer had hurried down to the canal bank the man had fled onto the main road. The labourer alerted two police officers, shouting to them that the man up ahead had just thrown a small boy into the canal.

The man was detained and strenuously denied the charge, and in doing so he made several attempts to strike his accuser. The man gave his name as John Horner of nearby Lissadel Street and claimed he was on his way home after spending the day in town. One of the officers went to the canal bank to check out the man's story while Horner was held on suspicion and taken to Salford police station.

Within the hour they had located the body of a young boy. A post-mortem found that he had been violently sodomised before being thrown into the water. Horner was placed in an identity parade where he was identified by Norman's friend Eric Wilson, and the two witnesses who had seen them on the canal bank.

Charged with the wilful murder, so great was the feeling of anger towards the prisoner that police feared Horner would be lynched and extra security was laid on at the remand hearing held the following day. He was tried at Manchester Assizes before Mr Justice Calvert on 11 July. The prosecution's case was built primarily on the testimony of eyewitnesses. They claimed that Horner was a pervert who gained his lust through cruelty.

The defence initially maintained that their client was innocent and that it was a case of mistaken identity. They claimed Horner was of previous good character – ignoring his long criminal record – and that he had enlisted in the Royal Navy at the age of 16, and fought bravely in the war until his discharge soon after the Armistice. When the defence realised things were going badly they concentrated on convincing the jury Horner was insane. Evidence was heard relating to the break up of his engagement and the question of his sanity. It was suggested that Horner had returned home from the war with a marked change in his character, after he had witnessed something that had a profound effect on him. The court also heard that, for no reason, he had struck out at his fiancée as she stood chatting with friends, and as she fell to the ground in tears he begged her forgiveness, claiming he didn't know what had come over him. As this had happened once before she decided to break off their engagement.

The jury took just a short time to find Horner guilty and, somewhat surprisingly, there was no immediate appeal against the sentence, as throughout the trial Horner had steadfastly maintained his innocence. In the condemned cell Horner put on over a stone in weight, 'grief fat' as it was known, and with the date for his execution fast approaching he announced that he now wished to appeal. He even wrote to his mother to tell her what he should like for his tea when he was released. It was all too late.

Outside the gaol on the morning of his execution a large crowd gathered. It included many members of the Pinchin family and they stood quietly in the warm sunshine. On the stroke of 8 a.m., as the bell began its mournful toll, a large cheer rang out. To the Pinchen family, and the people of Pendleton, justice was seen to have been done.

62

SPIRITUALISM

Patrick Power, 26 May 1925

'I wish to give myself up, I killed my landlady. I hit her on the head with a hammer. If she is not dead now she is near it and she deserved it'

Confession by Paddy Power, 11 April 1925.

At 3.30 p.m. on Saturday 11 April 1925, a man walked into Pendleton police station and confessed to the desk sergeant that he had killed his landlady. Detectives hurried round to the house on Whit Lane, Pendleton, where they discovered the body of 46-year-old Sarah Ann Sykes lying under a piano in the front sitting room, suffering from shock and bleeding heavily from a head wound. She was rushed to Salford Infirmary where she died shortly after admittance.

Tenant 41-year-old Patrick 'Paddy' Power was charged with the murder and sent for trial at Manchester Assizes on 8 May, where the story behind the brutal murder was explained to the court. Defended by Kenneth Burke, KC and a stalwart of pre-war Manchester murder trials, Power pleaded not guilty.

Outlining the case against the accused, the prosecution said it was a murder committed out of rage at being pressed to repay a debt. Power had called into the police station at Pendleton and confessed to murder. He was cautioned and detained while an investigation was carried out, but he had been sober when he confessed. Former soldier Power had lodged with the victim and her husband since December 1924, when he was discharged with an exemplary record after completing 23 years service in the military.

Up until the murder he had been on good terms with the landlady and her husband, but a few days before the murder, Power, who was claiming unemployment benefit, borrowed £5 from Mr Sykes and on the morning of the murder she was pressing for him to repay the money.

On the morning of 11 April, Power came down to breakfast and was reminded that he must repay the debt that day or face eviction. Shortly after lunch Mr Sykes, who worked as an ice-cream salesman, went out to work leaving Power and his wife in the house.

It was shortly after Sykes left the house that Power made his murderous attack. Mrs Sykes had suffered terrible injuries including three broken ribs, a skull fractured in seven places and a fractured jaw. The tip of her thumb had also been severed.

Power claimed that he couldn't remember carrying out the attack, but did recall coming to his senses and finding himself standing over his landlady's stricken body, and realising what he must have done he contacted the police.

Kenneth Burke told the court that Mrs Sykes was known locally as a spiritualist and a medium and suggested that Power may have been under the influence of spiritualism when he committed the crime. He said that powerfully built Power was a heavy drinker and it wouldn't have needed much effort to cause the injuries. He also suggested that Power was suffering from epilepsy, but it was all in vain.

Looking older than his 41 years, Power stood in silence as the jury returned after just ten minutes to find him guilty of murder. Once Mr Justice Finlay had sentenced him to death Power made no appeal and refused to sanction a movement to grant him a reprieve. Forty-eight days later he was led from his cell and executed.

63

IGNORANCE AND FEAR

James Makin, 11 August 1925

Twenty-five-year-old Jim Makin lost his job at a Manchester bleach works on 1 May 1925. He had not long been married and he and his wife rented a room at a house on Cross Street, Newton Heath, Manchester, from her uncle, and being upset at being out of work he spent the weekend getting drunk. He promised his wife he would find work on the Monday, but vows he made to look for a job were put on hold when he woke with a hangover and he decided to put it off until the following day.

Later that Monday afternoon, he called into his local pub for an afternoon drink. He had not long been settled in his seat when a young woman came over and began talking to him. He had spoken to her on the Friday night, but could not recall her name. As they chatted again he learned that she was 24-year-old Sarah 'Sadie' Clutton from Liverpool, and they got on so well that by closing time she asked him if he wanted to go for more drinks.

Makin by this time had discovered that Sadie was a prostitute and as they left the pub he told her he was going home and thanked her for her company. As he neared his home he was dismayed to find that she had followed him back, determined to procure a little business for herself. He told her to go away and entered the house, quickly closing the door behind him, but moments later there was a knock on the door – but hoping that she would go away, Makin ignored it. After several minutes of relentless knocking, he decided to see the woman off once and for all. Opening the door, he noticed that a shopkeeper across the street was watching intently through her window and so, not wanting to make a scene, he reluctantly admitted Sadie into his house.

At shortly after 5 p.m., Makin's wife returned home from work and made her way to her room where she discovered the body of a woman lying on the bed. The victim had severe bruising to the body, deep cuts to her face and neck, and three fingers on her left hand had been cut down to the bone. Beside the body was a bloodied carving knife, and glass from a broken beer bottle littered the room. Her horrified screams brought her uncle rushing from downstairs and, seeing that she was dead, he hurried to fetch the police.

Makin meanwhile had gone into Manchester city centre, where he ran into Arthur Green, an old friend, who was drinking in the Falstaff Hotel on Market Place. Makin invited Green to join him for a drink and he immediately confessed that he had killed a woman in his home. Makin then emptied his wallet onto the table and gave the money to Green saying that he had no use for it now as he was going to give himself up. He then caught a tram to Newton Heath and handed himself in at the police station.

The details behind the brutal murder were explained when Makin stood trial at Manchester Assizes on 25 July. The prosecution claimed that ignorance and fear were the cause of the brutal murder. Makin said that once the woman had forced her way into the house, they had more to drink before he agreed to have sex with her. They went upstairs and after sex he noticed that his penis was bloodstained. Sadie Clutton had been menstruating at the time, but in his naivety Makin believed he had caught a sexually transmitted disease.

He asked her if she had infected him and when she refused to answer and burst into tears, Makin picked up a bottle and struck her over the head, before cutting her throat. He had then changed his shirt and gone out into Manchester where he had confessed to his friend.

Any sympathies he may had garnered from the jury were destroyed when it was found that he often associated with prostitutes and, although he had been drunk at the time, and Sadie Clutton had all but forced herself upon him, that was no excuse for what was a shocking and brutal crime.

Prostitute Sadie Clutton (left) was murdered by Jim Makin (above). (T.J. Leech Archive)

Although the defence asked for a verdict of manslaughter due to extreme provocation, the fact that he had admitted he had left the bedroom to fetch a knife from the kitchen before cutting her throat suggested this was more than just a spur of the moment attack, and Mr Justice Wright told the jury that manslaughter was not an option open to them while considering their verdict.

64

THE GOOD-TIME GIRL

Samuel Johnson, 15 December 1925

Samuel Johnson had never tried to hide his past. Married with three children, he and his wife had separated two years before, and as 29-year-old Johnson had now fallen in love with 23-year-old Beatrice 'Betty' Philomena Martin, he made plans to get a divorce. Johnson had been courting Betty for the last year and was a regular visitor to her house on 13 Wingfield Street, Stretford, and even though her family knew of his past, they accepted him as a worthy suitor for their daughter.

In fact, Mr and Mrs Martin actively encouraged him at the house as they hoped he would make an honest woman of Betty, whom they felt was acting in a manner that brought shame both on herself and on them. The reason for this was that Betty spent a lot of time in the pubs along Trafford Road, close to the docks and a popular haunt for pimps and prostitutes. Although Betty wasn't a prostitute as such, she had no qualms about sailors lavishing money and drinks on her, and if she liked her companion enough, she would on occasion spend the night with him. She was really nothing more than a 'good-time girl', but once she met Johnson she tried to change her ways and made plans to settle down and get married once he was free to do so.

The relationship was going well until May 1925, when her attitude suddenly changed towards Johnson. She told him bluntly that she no longer wished to get married. He suspected that she had been spending time on Trafford Road again and discovered that she was seeing another man.

Johnson learned that the rival for her affections was a sailor named Jack Hunter, home on shore leave. Johnson turned up one night while they were in a pub close to her house and made such a scene that he was ordered out of the bar after making threats to both Betty and Hunter. Johnson took to calling at her house and making a nuisance of himself, to the extent that her father, who had previously shown fondness for Johnson, told him he was no longer welcome.

On the night of 26 July, Johnson called at her house and asked her to go for a drink with him. She refused, and when she later left the house he followed her and spent the night spying on her as she visited various bars around the docks. In the early hours he returned to her house and waited for her to arrive.

At 2 a.m. Betty arrived home with Hunter, who she kissed goodbye before walking up the path. She noticed Johnson waiting for her and they began to quarrel. Suddenly, and without warning, he pulled out a knife and stabbed her in the back. The screams attracted the attention of Jack, who hurried back to find Betty dead on the doorstep. As he walked up the path, Johnson pushed past him and said he was going to the police.

At his Manchester trial before Mr Justice Wright on 23 November, Johnson chose to plead guilty and refused any sort of legal aid, and once the judge was satisfied the prisoner understood the consequences of such an action, he proceeded to sentence him to death. The trial lasted just four minutes.

The day before his execution Johnson had refused to see his wife, but asked to see the hangman for five minutes on the eve of the execution because he did not want to upset him! The Governor told Johnson that he would see Mr Willis at one minute to eight and not before.

The following morning a crowd gathered at the prison gates as the bell tolled at 8 a.m. to signify that the execution had been carried out, and the newspapers that evening recorded this fact. Papers discovered recently record that the execution did not in fact take place until 11 a.m., by which time the crowd had dispersed believing that justice had already been done.

BLACK CAP DRAMA
OF
FOUR MINUTES.

Condemned Man Refuses to Defend Himself.

By Our Special Commissioner.

STRANGE glimpses of the working of the human mind are gained sometimes in courts of law, but never has there been, in this country, a more startling revelation of a man's character and strength than that which gripped all present in the Crown Court at Manchester Assizes, where Sam Johnson was called upon to answer a charge of having murdered Beatrice Philomena Martin at Stretford on July 27. The short, sturdily-built young fellow—Johnson is only 28 years of age—was before the Court for four minutes, but it was a time so charged with emotion that few could have said, immediately afterwards, how long had passed from the moment he stepped into the dock to that in which he returned to the cells, sentenced to death.

His fair hair was slightly rumpled, his clean-shaven face was flushed with suppressed excitement as he stood at the rail of the dock. The Clerk of Arraigns, Sir Herbert Stephen, read the magistrate's and the coroner's indictments. "Are you guilty or not guilty?" he asked. Johnson answered firmly: I plead guilty.

Replying to an inquiry by Mr. Justice Wright, the man said: "I don't want anyone to defend me. I refuse to be defended."

Beatrice Martin.

Left: *Newspaper account of the murder of Betty Martin.* (T.J. Leech Archive)

Below: *Johnson's request to meet hangman Willis before his execution was refused.* (T.J. Leech Archive)

The Illustrated Police News *account of the execution of Sam Johnson.* (T.J. Leech Archive)

TERRIBLE BOLTON CRIME.

Married Woman Murdered in Bedroom.

DRAMATIC ARREST OF SUSPECTED MAN.

Alleged Attempts at Suicide.

News cutting of the Bolton murder. (Author's Collection)

65

THE ONE-LEGGED WATCHMAN

William Henry Thorpe, 16 March 1926

William Thorpe cursed and drank, alone in his private grief, devastated that the woman he loved had married another man. Earlier in the summer when Frances Godfrey found herself pregnant she asked Thorpe to marry her, but he had refused, and she had wasted no time in finding someone who would marry her. William Clarke was prepared to marry the pregnant Frances and from then on she severed all contact with Thorpe. He tried to get her to change her mind, and even told her he would marry her, but it was all too late.

The 45-year-old one-legged ex-soldier – he had lost the lower part of a leg during the First World War – had moped around the building site at Breightmet, Bolton, where he worked as a labourer and watchman, and after collecting his weekly pay he headed straight for his local pub. On Thursday evening, 19 November 1925, Thorpe caught the trolley bus into Bolton town centre where he drowned his sorrows, before catching a bus back to the Hare and Hounds, where he finished the night off.

He ordered a bottle of rum at closing time and staggered home to his lodgings at 1 Crompton Fold, Breightmet, and throughout the night he drank and brooded. As first light broke, he decided that if he couldn't have Frances then no one would.

Thirty-nine-year-old Frances Clarke, née Godfrey, shared a small terrace house with her new husband and her 70-year-old mother on Clarke Street, in the Victory district of Bolton. At 5 a.m. on Friday morning, William Clarke left home for work, leaving Frances asleep in the back bedroom. Less than an hour later, Frances' mother was woken by a piercing scream coming from the adjacent room. As the old woman sat up in bed she heard a familiar thumping noise coming from her staircase – as though someone was attempting to make a quick exit. She rushed towards Frances' room and, opening the door, she recoiled in horror at the sight of her daughter lying on the bed with a terrible gash to her throat. As blood pumped freely from the gaping wound Frances whispered a name to her mother, 'Thorpe!'

Assistance was quickly summoned; the fire-station ambulance hurried from nearby Marsden Road, but by the time it had rattled down the cobbled street Frances Clarke was dead. A murder inquiry was immediately set up and by lunchtime Thorpe was in custody. Thorpe told detectives as he was placed under arrest that he was planning to cut his own throat, having made a number of unsuccessful attempts to kill himself that morning: firstly he had tried to throw himself under the wheels of a tram as he escaped from the scene of the crime, but due to the weather the tram was only crawling so the driver was able to brake and avoid hitting him; he had then jumped from the cab and angrily remonstrated with Thorpe, who responded by pushing him to the ground and disappearing into the thick fog that enveloped the town. Later that morning Thorpe had tried to drown himself in a nearby canal, but being unable to hold his head under the water he had returned home, and had been about to draw the razor across his throat when the door burst open and he was placed under arrest.

Thorpe's trial opened before Mr Justice Wright at Manchester on 23 February 1926. His defence was that drink had rendered him insane. In his summing up, which seemed to side with the defence, Mr Justice Wright said that in some cases people who were very drunk were insane. Addressing the jury he said that they all knew from sad experience that drunkenness did weaken a man's self-control and, as a result, he very often did things he would not do when sober, and in some cases a man may be so drunk as not to be able to form the necessary intention to commit a crime. But was this insanity?

The jury needed just thirty minutes to find the prisoner guilty of murder, but added a strong recommendation for mercy. Thorpe stood unmoved as the death sentence was passed. Numerous petitions were organised in an attempt to secure a reprieve. One petition in Blackpool, Thorpe's birthplace, collected over 7,000 names and similar numbers were collected at his former workplace and in many of Bolton town-centre pubs, but four days before the date scheduled for his execution the Home Secretary announced that the appeal had failed and Thorpe must die.

66

DEAD MAN'S BOOTS

Louie Calvert, 24 June 1926

Although small and unattractive, 33-year-old Louie Calvert, using the name Louie Gomersal, worked the streets of Leeds with a fair degree of success. She had had several aliases, and to the Salvation Army, whose meetings she attended regularly, she was known as Louise Jackson. She also had a violent temper and more than one client had received a beating when they tried to avoid payment for her 'services'.

It was under the name of Louise Jackson that she had taken a position as live-in housekeeper to nightwatchman Arthur Calvert early in 1925. Calvert lived on Railway Place in the Pottery Fields area of Leeds, and welcomed both Louie and her young son into the house. Soon Calvert and his housekeeper began a relationship and in due course she told him she was pregnant. It was a lie.

She persuaded Calvert to marry her and for a while was able to deceive him regarding her condition until she realised she would have to do something to convince him she was telling the truth. She packed her bags and told him she was going to stay with sister in Dewsbury during her confinement. She was in Dewsbury long enough to send a telegram confirming her arrival before returning to Leeds to carry on her career as a prostitute.

On 8 March 1926, she took lodgings with Lily Waterhouse, a 40-year-old eccentric widow, who lived on Amberley Road, Leeds. They came to an arrangement whereupon Louie would act as housekeeper in return for her board and lodging. A week later she saw an advert for a child to be adopted and agreed to adopt the baby girl from an unmarried teenage mother. She arranged to collect the baby on 31 March and notified her husband of the planned date of her return home.

Soon Mrs Waterhouse began to suspect that personal items and silverware were going missing, and when she discovered a pawnshop ticket she was convinced her housekeeper was stealing from her. On 30 March she reported her suspicions to the police and when Louie came home later she confronted her with her suspicions.

The police had made an appointment with magistrates for 1 April and on the evening of 31 March she was seen by her neighbours entering her house. At 7.30 p.m. neighbours heard sounds of banging and crying coming from the house and a few minutes later Louie departed with the new baby. When a neighbour enquired about the crying, Louie told her Mrs Waterhouse was upset because she was leaving and she had left her weeping in bed.

When Mrs Waterhouse failed to turn up for the court appointment two officers were detailed to investigate. They called at the house and when they were unable to rouse the occupant the neighbour came out and mentioned the crying and sounds of disturbances. The officers obtained a spare key and discovered the body of Mrs Waterhouse lying dead in a small bedroom at the top of the stairs. She had been strangled and beaten around the head, but there was no sign of a break in or a struggle. Curiously, the dead woman's boots were missing.

There was only one suspect and Louie Calvert was soon traced to her husband's house in Leeds. She greeted the officers when they called wearing a pair of boots several sizes too big for her. A search of her belongings also recovered many of the items Mrs Waterhouse had reported as missing from her home.

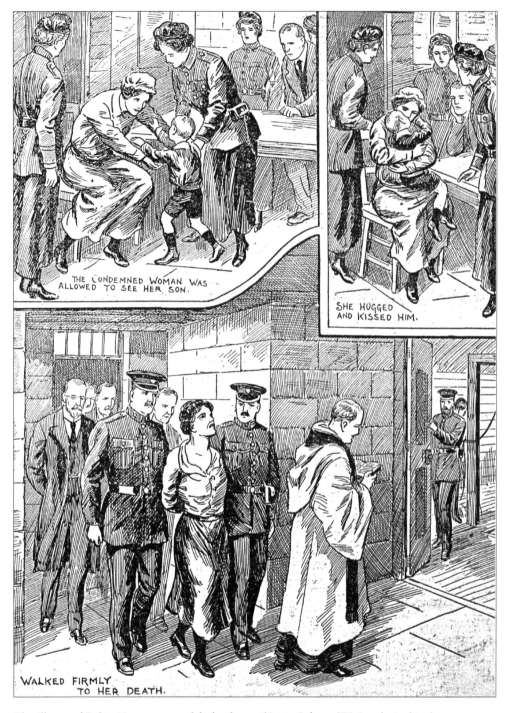

THE CONDEMNED WOMAN WAS ALLOWED TO SEE HER SON.

SHE HUGGED AND KISSED HIM.

WALKED FIRMLY TO HER DEATH.

The Illustrated Police News *account of the last hours of Louie Calvert.* (T.J. Leech Archive)

She denied committing murder and at Leeds Assizes before Mr Justice Wright on 5 May she pleaded not guilty. Calvert's claims that all the items found in her possession had been given to her by the dead woman were exposed as a pack of lies and on the second day of the trial the jury took just a short time to find her guilty.

Asked if she had anything to say as to why sentence of death should not be passed on her, she said, 'Yes, I am pregnant!'

Known as 'pleading her belly', in the Victorian days, this would have meant the execution was postponed until the birth of the child. The execution would then usually be carried out a week or so later, but in the new century the unwritten law was that a woman would be granted a reprieve.

For some reason the execution was scheduled to take place at Strangeways where she was examined by prisoner doctors. They could find no signs of pregnancy, although they did say if she was it was the earliest stages and would not prevent her being executed. Despite this, a petition for a reprieve gained 3,000 signatures and questions were even asked in parliament asking if the execution should go ahead. On Tuesday 22 June, the Home Office issued a statement saying the execution would go ahead and there was no truth in the story of her being pregnant.

Awaiting the hangman, Calvert confessed to another murder in 1922. Then she was using the name Louise Jackson and had worked as the housekeeper to one John Frobisher of Mercy Street, Leeds. On 12 July that year he was found by a policeman floating face down in a canal, and a post-mortem found he had been battered about the head and suffered a fractured skull. Although the housekeeper had been questioned several times with regards to the suspected murder, the coroner later recorded a verdict of misadventure. Frobisher's boots had been missing when his body was recovered from the water.

Her 6-year-old son, Kenneth, to whom she was devoted, was allowed to visit her on the day before her execution, and she was also visited by her husband who she had deceived so coldly before the murder.

At a few minutes to 8 a.m. on Thursday 24 June, the hangmen stood outside the condemned cell at the end of 'B' wing waiting for the signal to enter. An hour later an autopsy was carried out which found that death had been due to dislocation of the cervical vertebrae. It also found that, contrary to her plea, Mrs Calvert had not been pregnant.

67

THE BONFIRE NIGHT MURDER

Frederick Fielding, 3 January 1928

'I've a murder to do and I have come to buy a knife!' The staff in the ironmonger's shop on Rishton's High Street assumed he was just making a joke in poor taste, and having handed over the money the customer exited the shop. A week later newspaper headlines told them it had been no idle boast.

On Saturday evening, 5 November 1927, 23-year-old Eleanor Pilkington left her home in Rishton and met up with two sisters, Evelyn and Doris Walker, who lived a few doors away on Spring Street. The three of them had tickets for a Bonfire Night Dance at Mercer Hall in nearby Great Harwood. When the dance finished they caught the bus home, alighting 100 yards from Eleanor's home.

As they approached Spring Street they spotted Eleanor's former boyfriend, 24-year-old Fred Fielding, approaching. Eleanor told Doris to ignore him and moved to walk past, but Fielding barred the way.

'I want to speak to you Ellie,' he said, grabbing her arm and leading her into a shop doorway, but she shrugged off his grip and rejoined her friends. They started to walk down Spring Street when suddenly Fielding grabbed Eleanor by the shoulder, spun her round and stabbed her twice in the breast. Her friends managed to get Eleanor into the Walkers' house, which was just a few doors away, but she died before a doctor could be called.

Fielding had fled into the night. A murder inquiry was launched and a hunt for the killer began, but Fielding surrendered to a policeman within the hour in Blackburn, and confessed to him that he had just stabbed his girlfriend.

On 22 November 1927, at Manchester Assizes before Mr Justice Finlay, the details of the tragedy were told to the court. The couple had been courting for four years and they had discussed marriage. Then, in the summer of 1927, he announced he was quitting his job as a moulder in an iron foundry and joining the Metropolitan Police Force. He promised he would do all he could to keep their relationship going and during the three months training in London he returned home to see Ellie on a couple of occasions.

After three months' probation, he decided against a career in the police force and returned to his hometown of Clayton-le-Moors in September 1927. He had also missed seeing Ellie, but a week after he returned north she dropped the bombshell that she was ending their relationship. Fielding had secured his old job back in the foundry, but he was soon dismissed when he took to drinking heavily and changed from a hard-working young man into little more than a drunken layabout. He also lost his home and he decided that the cause of all his woes was Eleanor Pilkington.

He tried to get her to rekindle their romance, but when she refused he took to threatening her at her home, throwing stones at her window and demanding that she come out and speak to him. At the end of October he called at her house and again demanded to speak to her. Her father told him to go away and Fielding threatened that if he didn't let him speak to her he would be without a daughter before the week was out.

Those threats and the boast when he purchased the knife formed the basis of the prosecution's considerable evidence of premeditation. Fielding claimed that he had been so drunk that he had not known what he was doing, but had seemed lucid enough when he confessed to the policeman an hour after committing the murder. The jury took just fifteen minutes to decide that Fielding was guilty of murder.

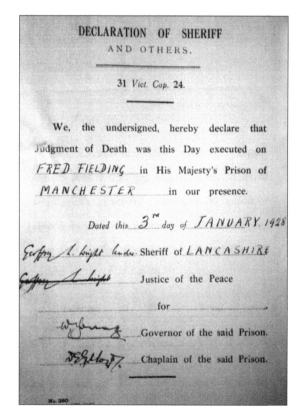

Above: *Fred Fielding.* (Author's Collection)

Left: *Notice of Fielding's execution.* (Author's Collection)

FIELDING PAYS THE PENALTY.

EXECUTED AT STRANGEWAYS.

LAST ACT IN RISHTON CRIME.

Fielding pays the penalty.
(Author's Collection)

68

THE MAN WITH THE GUN

Walter Brooks, 28 June 1928

On 20 August 1925 market salesman Walter Brooks was diagnosed as being temporarily insane after making unreasonable threats and accusations against his wife Beatrice. A three-day order that would commit him to an institution was issued the following day, but when Dr William Pimblett, the medical officer at Preston Prison who had signed the order, visited Brooks at his home on Grimshaw Street, Preston – and after reassurances from his wife that he had calmed down – the warrant was withdrawn.

In 1927, after two years of further matrimonial unrest, the marriage of twenty-six years ended. Beatrice and their two children, along with lodgers who had shared their house on Grimshaw Street, moved to a new house at 39 Avenham Road, while Walter Brooks took lodgings on Tithebarn Street.

One of the lodgers at Avenham Road was 50-year-old Alfred Moore, two years older than both Brooks and his wife, and Brooks soon came to the conclusion that Moore was to blame for his marriage ending, as he was having an affair with Beatrice.

Brooks obtained a service revolver from a fellow market trader and, on Wednesday 4 April 1928, as the pair approached their front door, Brooks emerged from a dark alley, shouted, 'I'll get you now', and fired at his wife and Moore. A passing police constable saw the flash from the gun and hurried to offer assistance. Moore lay slumped on the ground, mortally wounded, while the officer managed to get Beatrice Brooks home from where he summoned an ambulance. Moore died on the way to hospital and Mrs Brooks succumbed to her injuries later in hospital.

Brooks was soon under arrest and at his trial before Mr Justice Charles at Manchester Assizes on 8 May, the defence never questioned that Brooks had fired the fatal shots, but maintained that he had done so while insane. Evidence from the doctor who had issued the committal warrant in 1925 was heard in court and the jury heard of the long history of insanity in the Brooks family. Crucially, when Dr Pimblett was called to give evidence he said that, although he may have believed Brooks was suffering from temporary insanity in 1925, there was nothing in his behaviour since arrest to show insanity.

Concluding their case the prosecution said they believed that Brooks was faking insanity as a defence for a brutal double murder carried out because he believed his wife, who had recently ended their marriage, was having an affair with the lodger. The jury agreed there was no insanity and found him guilty as charged.

69

ORIENTAL HONEYMOON

Chung Yi Miao, 6 December 1928

It was in the autumn of 1927 that 28-year-old Chung Yi Miao, a Chinese law graduate, met 29-year-old Wai Sheung Siu, the daughter of a wealthy Chinese merchant, in New York. After a brief courtship they married in March 1928 and the newlyweds decided to honeymoon in the picturesque English Lake District. Crossing the Atlantic by liner they arrived first in Scotland before making their way south and arriving at the Borrowdale Gates Hotel, on the southern tip of Derwentwater, on 18 June.

The following morning the couple went for a walk around the lake and, after lunch at the hotel, they left again for an afternoon stroll. At 4 p.m. Miao returned to the hotel alone and retired to his room, after telling guests that his wife had gone shopping in nearby Keswick. He later came down for tea alone and seemed uncomfortable when guests questioned him over the whereabouts of his wife. He just repeated she had found the temperature rather chilly and had gone to Keswick to buy warmer clothes.

Miao was still eating his evening meal when the mystery of his wife's whereabouts was solved: at 7.30 p.m. a farmer discovered her body partially hidden beneath an umbrella beside Kidham Dub, a small bathing hole not far from the hotel. She had been punched in the mouth – her lip was split, leaving a trail of blood down her chin – and she had been strangled with three pieces of string and the cord from a blind. From the position of her clothes it appeared she had been raped or sexually assaulted. Missing from her fingers were her wedding and engagement rings.

When police officers called at the hotel to inform Miao of the discovery of the body later that night, he had already retired to bed. He was asked to accompany them to the local police station and when interviewed the following morning he made a fatal slip up, incriminating himself immediately by admitting that he knew she had been assaulted and robbed. Up until that point the detective had merely informed him that she had been found dead.

Evidence against him quickly began to pile up. A piece of white cord was found in the hotel room which matched exactly that found tied around her neck. In the wardrobe was Miao's brown overcoat, which he was known to have been wearing the previous afternoon. On close inspection it was found to be stained with human blood, and in a drawer two rolls of photographic film were found. They seemed to be harmless holiday snaps, but a detective picked the films up and handed them to the police photographer to see if they contained any clues in the photographs. In the laboratory one of the film containers was opened – and out spilled the two missing rings. Miao was arrested and charged with the murder of his wife.

When Miao stood trial before Mr Justice Humphreys at Carlisle on 22 November, the prosecution's case consisted mainly of circumstantial evidence. Miao had been seen walking with his wife and then she was found strangled by a piece of cord identical to one found in his hotel room. Her rings had been taken from the body and these too had been found concealed in the film canister in Miao's room. Detectives had also found a letter among his belongings that seemed to show that he planned to commit murder. It contained a few ramblings but ended with, 'don't do it on the ship, consider on arrival in Europe.' The prosecution alleged 'it' meant murder.

Miao's defence was a denial of the murder which he suggested may have been carried out by two Oriental men he claimed had been following them since they boarded the ship in New York. Witnesses were found who had seen two Chinese men in Keswick on the day of the murder, but they were never traced, and as it was a popular destination in the height of holiday season it was just put down to coincidence. On the third day of the trial the jury needed just one hour to decide he was guilty and asked if he had anything to say. Miao, in broken English, began to criticise the judge and the police for the way they had handled the case. He was eventually interrupted and the sentence of death was passed on him. Miao used his legal training to handle his own appeal, but it was in vain and was quickly rejected.

Although there was no doubt as to his guilt, detectives could not find a clear motive for why he would bring his wife on their honeymoon to the picturesque lakes and commit a brutal murder. He would stand to inherit from his wife's wealthy family, but that would be a long time in the future. They also pondered why he had not chosen to kill her in their homeland – perhaps he feared the rope less than the electric chair?

Shortly after his execution a Sunday newspaper printed what they alleged was Miao's confession. In the article it said that soon after they had married she found it was impossible for her to have sex, and although she had an operation to remedy this it was discovered that she would be unable to bear children. He had resorted to murder when he learned this, as he planned to find another wife who could bear him children. The article also claimed that on the eve of his execution, Miao had confessed to his warders and pulled out a £20 he had secreted about his person since arrest!

Chung Yi Miao and his bride. (Author's Collection)

70

A QUESTION OF INSANITY

George Henry Cartledge, 4 April 1929

Shortly before 9 a.m. on Wednesday 2 January 1929, a neighbour passing the house at 2 Oak Street, Shaw, saw an arm waving through an upstairs window. She called out asking if everything was alright, only for 25-year-old Nellie Cartledge to appear at the window and shout for her to call the police and fetch an ambulance.

By the time police officers had arrived, Mrs Cartledge was lying dead on the bedroom floor having suffered horrific throat wounds. On the floor beside her was a bloodstained razor and sitting on the bed was her husband, 27-year-old George Cartledge.

'I must have hit the missus,' was all he could say before being taken into custody. At the station Cartledge claimed he did not know what he had done and it was only when their 6-year-old daughter heard her mother crying and asked him why his hands were full of blood that he went back upstairs and discovered he had attacked his wife.

Cartledge was well known to police officers in Shaw and the surrounding area. He had worked sporadically as a navvy since his discharge from the army in 1919, but he was often out of work and spent most of his time drinking. He also had a string of convictions for assaulting tram drivers and policemen. He had married Nellie in 1921 and they had four children, but they lived in squalid conditions and six months before the murder the police had been called to the house when he had tried to strangle his wife. No charges had been made following the attempted assault.

At his Manchester Assizes trial in February, Cartledge offered a defence of insanity. He claimed he was suffering from head pains and was unaware of what had happened at the house on the morning of the murder. In December 1928 Cartledge had visited a doctor complaining of severe headaches and saying he was having trouble concentrating and sleeping. Three days before the murder he had gone back to the doctor who recorded that he found Cartledge much improved since his first visit.

The medical officer at Strangeways, Dr Shannon, told the court that the prisoner was below average intelligence and that he had made an unsuccessful attempt to commit suicide while at the prison. The doctor added that although he was of low intelligence and a neurasthenic, he did not believe he was in any way insane.

In a court of law the rule has always been that the defendant is innocent until proven guilty, but with insanity it is the other way around. Trail judge Mr Justice Finlay told the jury that the prosecution's case had clearly shown that Cartledge had been shown to be guilty of murder, but it boiled down to a question of sanity. He said that the onus was on the defence to prove that the prisoner was insane. If they believed he was, they could find him guilty but insane; if they didn't believe he was insane he would be guilty of murder.

They believed the latter, that he was guilty of wilful murder, but added a strong recommendation for mercy. A petition was raised in Shaw, but attracted little attention. Few mourned Cartledge, whose wicked murder had deprived four young children of both their parents, when he went to the gallows.

71

A FATAL MISTAKE

Francis Land, 16 April 1931

After a marriage lasting six years, 24-year-old Sarah Ellen 'Nellie' Johnson had had enough. Leaving her husband in January 1930 she soon took up with Francis Land, a 40-year-old boiler fireman who lived at Waterhouse Place, Rochdale. Soon the age difference between them began to tell, not helped by Land's intemperate and violent habits, and they began to spend most of their time quarrelling.

After another violent quarrel, in which Land gave her a fearful beating, on 2 December Nellie packed her bags and went to a friend's house. According to the friend, a Mrs Barlow, Nellie had a bruised jaw and there were bruises on her neck as if someone had attempted to strangle her. Nellie remained with Mrs Barlow for just the one night, before moving to stay with another friend, Emily Whitehead, and on 6 December they both went to stay with Emily's brother at 129 Oldham Road.

That night, the two women were drinking in the Flying Horse when Land spotted them in the lounge bar. Much the worse for drink, he was waiting for them when they left the pub and asked Nellie to come home with him. In no uncertain terms she told him he had struck her for the last time and she had no intentions of going back with him. Land then made a drunken threat to murder her if she turned him down again.

It was something of a surprise to her friends when, on Friday 12 December, Nellie agreed to meet Land to try and reconcile their differences. It was a fatal mistake. Nellie told Land she would return to him on condition he found a job outside Rochdale and away from his friends, who she thought were leading him astray. At 9 p.m. that night they were seen strolling arm-in-arm, and she was last seen heading back to his house.

At 9.30 p.m. Land arrived alone at the Rochdale Social Club, where he downed a quick drink. In the company of a friend he went to another public house, where the friend noticed that Land seemed quite distressed, but would not elaborate on the cause. When Nellie failed to return home following her meeting with Land, Emily went looking for her. She eventually called into the Grapes and saw Land at the bar. When she asked him what had happened to Nellie, Land replied that he had done her in. She called two men over and asked them to detain Land while she went to find a policeman. In the company of a police constable they returned to Waterhouse Place, where they discovered Nellie lying still in a pool of blood on the hearthrug. Death had clearly been due to the gaping throat wound.

At his three-day trial before Mr Justice Charles at Manchester Assizes, which began on 23 February, Land claimed he had an alibi for the time of the murder and had not been home since 5 p.m. that evening. Although several of his friends supported this alibi, there was the evidence of the woman who had seen Land and Nellie walking towards his house, and more crucially the verbal confession Land had made to Emily Whitehead.

His appeal on the grounds that the jury had been misdirected was heard at the end of March, but quickly rejected. Land's execution was the first one at Strangeways timed to take place at 9 a.m. rather than 8 a.m., but it was not made known in advance and the large crowd that had gathered at 8 a.m. had an extra hour to wait. Among those waiting for notification that the execution had been carried out was a group of children from the nearby school, and at a few moments to the appointed hour their headmaster joined the crowd trying to get the children into school.

One man in the crowd told reporters that this was the twentieth execution he had been present at at Strangeways, and that he had travelled all the way from Barrow-in-Furness just to stand at the prison gates.

72

ON HIS TWENTY-FIRST BIRTHDAY

Solomon Stein, 15 December 1931

I believe you were at the gate last night waiting to see me. It is about time you stopped this bunkum... I know quite well you hate me... and I have had to put up with it for twenty years. In the short time I have been in here it has been like heaven compared to the life I led with your barmy lot... I don't want to be bothered by you wanting to see me... please let me die in peace.

Letter penned by Solomon Stein to his parents, 14 December 1931.

The courtroom was stunned. The prisoner had just effectively sealed his own fate and put his own neck in the noose. When asked by the clerk of the court how the prisoner wished to plead, Counsel Mr Neville Laski stood up and said loudly, 'not guilty.' Then, to the shock of all present, the prisoner, Solomon Stein, jumped to his feet and shouted, 'Guilty! I wish to plead guilty.'

It was Wednesday 25 November 1931, and faced with such an outburst the trial judge asked the counsel to consult with his client to be sure he understood the gravity of such a plea. After a short recess, Laski confirmed that Stein did indeed wish to offer a guilty plea and moments later, with a black cap placed on his wig, Mr Justice Finlay sentenced the young man to death.

On Sunday morning, 4 October, the body of a woman was found in room number six at the Station Temperance Hotel, adjacent to Victoria Railway Station, Manchester. She had been strangled with a brown necktie. Detectives learned that on the previous night a man and woman had checked in and signed the register as Mr and Mrs Stanley. Stanley paid 10s and asked to be called at 8 a.m. the following morning. As it turned out the alarm call was not needed: shortly before 8 a.m. a maid saw Stanley leaving the hotel alone. There was no movement from room number six and with the check-out time now passed the cleaner took out a pass key and, letting herself in, she discovered the body of a woman lying on the bed.

From papers in her possession, 'Mrs Stanley' was identified as 28-year-old Annie Riley of Camp Street, Deansgate. Annie Riley worked as a city-centre prostitute and her friends told officers they had seen her in the company of a man the previous night and were able to give them a detailed description of him. A hunt began.

The following afternoon the search for the killer ended when Solomon Stein, a Jewish waterproof machinist from Hightown, Salford, surrendered to the police and confessed to carrying out the murder.

Stein said that 3 October was his twenty-first birthday and he had gone to the Theatre Royal cinema, leaving at around half past ten. He had spotted Annie Riley at the corner of Market Street and Cross Street. They chatted and she agreed to spend the night with him, if he paid for the hotel room.

At 6 a.m. the following morning, Stein claimed that he woke and started to get dressed. Checking his belongings, he found he was missing 15s. Believing Annie might have stolen it, he picked up his tie – and before he realised what he was doing he had strangled her. After leaving the hotel he went home, ate breakfast and then went to work, though he left after just a few minutes. He then spent much of the day walking around. Eventually he headed towards the hotel near Victoria Station where he saw a small crowd gathered. The following morning he bought himself a paper, and after reading about his crime he decided to give himself up.

Stein refused his parents permission to visit him in the condemned cell, even going as far as to write them a long letter when they turned up at the prison on the day before he was to hang. He refused their last requests for a visit, and in the letter he effectively disowned them: he added that he hoped all his relatives would end their lives on Devil's Island.

A crowd of over 1,500 Jews gathered outside the prison gates in the drizzling rain waiting for the notice of execution to be posted. It was reported in the papers that just five seconds elapsed from the pinioning of the prisoner to the drop falling.

73

ATTEMPTED RAPE

George Alfred Rice, 3 February 1932

The search for 9-year-old Constance Inman went on until darkness fell; then, reluctantly, it was abandoned until first light. Connie had last been seen alive by her friend, 10-year-old Olga Roberts, at 6.30 p.m. on the evening of Tuesday 22 September 1931, when Olga saw her playing on Victoria Park, Rusholme, Manchester. Half an hour later, when Connie failed to return home for her tea, her parents organised a search of the area before contacting the police.

The following morning a domestic worker drew the curtains at a house on Park Range and spotted what looked like a large doll lying in some bushes in the garden of a house on Dickenson Road. Going to investigate she found she had discovered the body of Constance Inman.

Detectives soon found that the young girl had died from asphyxiation and from the marks on her neck it appeared she had been strangled. Her clothing was disturbed and it appeared she had been the victim of a violent sexual assault. It was also clear that she had been murdered elsewhere and her body dumped in the garden.

Inquiries led police to believe that the killer may be the man several children had reported hanging around in the area in the days before the murder, and they also discovered that Connie had mentioned meeting a man who had promised to give her some cigarette cards.

Routine police enquires led them to 97 Dickenson Road, where officers spoke to a one-eyed lodger who gave his name as Price. He claimed he had been at the cinema on the night Connie disappeared, and after taking a routine statement the officers moved on. However, the following day, after interviewing Annie Broadhurst, the landlady at 97 Dickenson Road, detectives decided to speak to Price again. Mrs Broadhurst had mentioned two facts that the officers found interesting.

Firstly, she said Price had discussed Connie's death and seemed quite knowledgeable on certain facts. When asked how he knew these details, Price told her he had read about it in the local paper. This she found hard to believe, as she knew the tenant was illiterate. Secondly, she had heard a noise the night before Connie was discovered which sounded like Price was dragging something heavy along the corridor.

Questioned again, Price now admitted that his name was George Alfred Rice and that he was a 32-year-old out of work labourer. He offered an alibi for the night Connie disappeared, claiming he was at the cinema all evening, and had gone to bed when he returned home. When he was asked for proof of his visit to the cinema he produced a stub that was six months out of date, and he was taken into custody pending further enquiries. Rice was questioned again at length at the station and finally admitted he was involved in Connie's death.

'Give me a cup of tea and I will tell you all about it', he told officers at the station, before saying that he had met up with Connie at around 6.30 p.m. and while he was giving her a cuddle she had collapsed to the ground. In a panic he had fled and gone to the cinema and when he returned he was horrified to find her lying where he had left her. He panicked and then hid her body where it was later discovered.

When Rice stood trial before Mr Justice Finlay at Manchester Assizes on 14 December, his counsel claimed that while he had admitted being responsible for the death of Constance Inman, it had been an accident and the charge should be one of manslaughter.

The prosecution claimed that it was only accidental inasmuch as Connie was suffocated while Rice was attempting to rape her, and that as she had died as a result of his actions it was murder and not manslaughter.

The harrowing evidence of the attempted rape was relayed in court and at the end of his two-day trial Rice's fate hinged on whether the jury believed that Constance had been raped or not. The judge directed them that if he had raped her, or had intended to rape her, he was guilty of murder. If, however, the jury thought that he was guilty of merely an indecent assault they could return a verdict of manslaughter.

The jury returned after forty minutes of deliberation with a verdict of guilty of murder. Rice collapsed as the sentence of death was passed, and Mr Justice Finlay, feeling the strain of the trial, wept as he passed sentence.

The day before his execution, friends visited Rice in the condemned cell and he told them that he would die bravely. It was a idle boast, for when Tom Pierrepoint entered his cell on the stroke of eight, he broke down completely and had to be carried, an inert and broken man, to the gallows.

74

CHILD-KILLER

Charles James Cowle, 18 May 1932

There was no doubt that he was guilty of the dreadful sex murder of a 6-year-old girl, but despite the disgusting nature of the crime, there was a great attempt to get the killer reprieved. Roy Calvert, a well-known abolitionist and chairman of the National Council for the Abolition of the Death Penalty, told the national press it was outrage that a 'mental defective' with the mental age of not much older than his victim could be convicted and hanged based on insanity laws that were drafted in 1843 and were obsolete and not reflective of modern times.

Six-year-old Naomi 'Annie' Farnworth had finished morning lessons at Highfield Infants and along with other children made her way to nearby Vernon School for her school dinner, a lunch of potato hash. She was seen soon afterwards, with one of her friends, at half past twelve, in a local fish and chip shop carrying a large white jug. It was Tuesday 22 March 1932.

By 6.30 p.m., when Annie had still not returned to her home on Kay Street, Darwen, her parents began making enquiries in the neighbourhood. With each search drawing a blank the police were called; the following evening neighbours formed search parties to comb the nearby woods.

On Thursday morning detectives called at 18-year-old Charlie Cowle's house, a few doors along the street from Annie's, and told him that they had information that the young girl had run an errand for him on the day she disappeared, and that the white jug she had been carrying when last seen belonged to him. He admitted that she had run an errand for him and that he had asked her to go to Brumfitt's for tripe and chips. He said that she had returned with his lunch and had gone on to school. They asked to search his house. Upstairs they saw a large tin trunk, to which Cowle immediately pointed. He confessed that Annie was inside and that he had strangled her.

When her body was removed for a post-mortem it was found that she had been raped and strangled and that her stomach contained the school meal of potato hash along with some chips she had fetched for Cowle's lunch and which she had presumably shared.

Cowle stood trial before Mr Justice Humphreys at Manchester Assizes on 26 April. There was little doubt that he was the murderer and his counsel tried to show he was insane. Evidence was shown that Cowle had been sent to borstal at the age of nine following the attempted murder of a 2-year-old boy. Cowle claimed that before the attack on Annie he had felt a funny feeling in his head.

Combating the evidence of insanity, the prison's medical officer said he had studied the prisoner at length following his arrest and could find no signs of insanity and that Cowle appeared perfectly rational.

Believing the prisoner to be insane, the judge instructed the jury there could only be two verdicts in this case: guilty or guilty while insane. The jury took just fifteen minutes to believe Cowle was sane and he was condemned to death.

Following a consultation with the trial judge the appeal panel ordered a medical inquiry. Again it found that Cowle was neither insane nor mentally defective, and despite him still being a month short of his nineteenth birthday he was returned to the death cell to await the hangman.

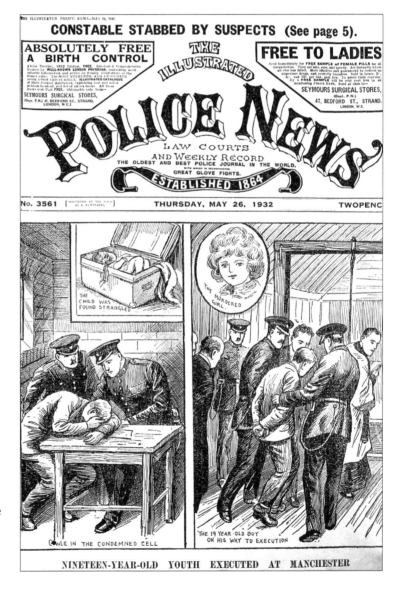

The Illustrated Police News *account of the execution of the Darwen child killer.* (T.J. Leech Archive)

75

THE CONFESSION

William Burtoft, 19 December 1933

Shortly after lunchtime on Wednesday 19 July 1933, 61-year-old widow Mrs Frances Levine, a wealthy Jewess, was found battered to death at her home at 453 Cheetham Hill Road, Cheetham Hill. Maid Freda Phillips told detectives that on her return from an errand she had seen Mrs Levine lying on the sofa in her living room and assumed she was having a nap. She busied herself with chores upstairs, but when she returned downstairs an hour later she noticed something was amiss: a bloodstained poker lay on the hearthrug – and on closer inspection she saw that Mrs Levine had horrific head wounds.

Frances Levine died later in hospital, and as detectives launched a murder inquiry they received the description of a man seen loitering about Cheetham Hill Road on the day of the murder. Police believed she had disturbed someone robbing the house and one week after the murder, 48-year-old Burtoft, a one-eyed, out-of-work sailor and meths drinker of no fixed abode, was arrested and taken into custody at Hyde charged with drunkenness. Burtoft fitted the description of the man wanted for the Cheetham Hill murder, and under questioning he at last confessed to committing the brutal crime. He made a statement that began, 'I admit being the murderer of Mrs Levine, owing to drinking methylated spirits ... '

At Burtoft's trial, before the recently appointed Mr Justice Atkinson on 13 November, his defence counsel claimed that the evidence against their client was, at best, suspect. Though Burtoft admitted he was in the area at the time, there was little other evidence, other than his 'confession', linking him to the crime.

Burtoft later withdrew this confession, claiming it had been made under duress. Questioned by the defence, a detective explained that Burtoft had made his statement during a thirty-minute period yet, when this statement was examined, it was found to contain a little over 200 words and could have been dictated in a fraction of that time. The wording was also suspicious: some of the language did not sound like the words a meths-drinking sailor would use. However, although the defence asked for this to be withdrawn from evidence, the judge allowed it to stay.

Mrs Levine's sitting room – note the blood-stained cushion on the sofa. (TNA:PRO)

The defence counsel also referred to the amount of blood and the frequency of the splashes found in the house. They reasoned that if Burtoft had been the killer his clothing would show traces of blood. No traces of blood were found on any of his clothes.

The prosecution agreed that the confession was the only real piece of evidence, and other than showing that Burtoft had spent a little money after the murder, when before he was known to be short, there was little else to connect him to the crime. His defence asked the jury to acquit the prisoner as there was no case to answer, but he was convicted on the evidence of his supposed confession, the jury evidently believing the police version of events, and with the jury finding Burtoft guilty it was left to Mr Justice Atkinson to pass his first death sentence.

76

ANOTHER GIRL

John Harris Bridge, 30 May 1935

They had been childhood sweethearts, and by the spring of 1935, 25-year-olds Amelia 'Millie' Nuttall and John Bridge had become engaged. They had even set a date for the wedding, 8 June 1935. Although Millie was still very much in love, Salford warehouseman Bridge seemed to have cooled on the relationship. He had even started to see another girl behind his fiancée's back.

Wishing to put things in the open he told Millie that he had another girl, Eileen Earl, who he had met at work, and wanted to break off their relationship. Although she now had a rival for his affections, Millie wasn't about to give up her sweetheart easily. She begged Bridge to reconsider his decision. When she burst into tears, he was unable to go through with the separation. Several times he made attempts to break up with her but each time she became hysterical and he hadn't the heart to continue.

On Sunday 14 April, Bridge spent the afternoon with Eileen before kissing her goodbye and going home for his tea. He had also arranged a meeting with Millie that evening as he planned to tell her once and for all that he was ending their engagement. No sooner had he arrived than she began to chastise him for being late and accusing him of being with the other girl. They began to quarrel, whereupon she picked up a poker and threatened him with it. Bridge tried to disarm her, and during the ensuing struggle he managed to snatch the poker and strike her across the head. As she slumped to the ground he picked up a bread knife and cut her throat, before rummaging through drawers and scattering contents across the floor to make it look like the work of a burglar. Bridge then returned to spend the evening with Eileen Earl.

Millie's father returned home at 10.15 p.m. and found the house in total darkness. He knew Millie was expecting her fiancé that evening and assumed he must have left and Millie gone to bed, but as soon as he turned up the lights he recoiled in horror. Amelia was lying dead on the kitchen floor among the scattered papers and upturned furniture.

Bridge arrived home later that night and was told there had been an 'accident' and the police wished to speak to him. At Salford police station he made a statement admitting that he had visited Amelia that evening, but claiming he had left her following a quarrel. Detectives did not believe his account, especially as there was no sign of forced entry (which discarded the burglar theory). Eventually he admitted that they had quarrelled and said that her death had been an accident.

When Bridge stood trial before Mr Justice Hilbery on 3 May, he again maintained her death was accidental. However, under cross examination he was forced to admit that he had cut her throat with the knife as she lay slumped on the floor following the blow by the poker. This destroyed his claims that he had struck her during a struggle and ultimately condemned him.

Bridge's execution marked the first visit to Manchester of wealthy abolitionist Mrs Violet Van der Elst, who organised protests outside the prison walls. Huge crowds had gathered at sunrise behind barricades police had put up to contain the crowds and prevent any protest getting too close to the gates. As the protesters arrived many of the crowd began to heckle Mrs Van der Elst, who had an angry exchange of words with many of the women as the hour of execution approached.

Crowds throng the streets outside the prison as Bridge is hanged. (Author's Collection)

Mrs Van der Elst fights her way through the crowd to protest at the execution of John Bridge in 1935.
(Author's Collection)

77

THE DEADLY DOCTOR

Buck Ruxton, 12 May 1936

Red stains on the carpet, red stains on the knife,
For Dr Buck Ruxton has murdered his wife:
The maid saw it and threatened to tell,
So Dr Buck Ruxton he killed her as well.

Contemporary children's rhyme from the 1930s.

On a warm Sunday afternoon, 29 September 1935, a young Edinburgh holidaymaker was taking a stroll down a country lane in Moffat, Dumfries. Reaching a small bridge crossing Gardenholm Linn, a tributary of the River Annan, she looked down and spotted a human arm wrapped in a newspaper, trapped between boulders in the fast-flowing waters.

Police officers soon organised a search of the scene and discovered further body parts, each wrapped in a separate sheet of newspaper. The search yielded over seventy different parts which were gathered up and transferred to a local hospital where the maggot-ridden, decomposing flesh was examined by Edinburgh-based Professor John Glaister and his staff.

Glaister was soon able to tell detectives that whoever had dismembered the bodies possessed a detailed anatomical knowledge as almost all traces of identification had been removed. He was also able to tell detectives that he was looking at the bodies of two females; one aged around forty, the other perhaps half that age. A search of missing people from the local area produced no leads; neither did the investigation when it was widened across the whole of Scotland.

On Tuesday 1 October, police in Lancaster received a visit from Mrs Jessie Rogerson, who informed them of the disappearance of her step-daughter, Mary, who worked as a live-in housemaid to a local doctor, Buck Ruxton. The worried stepmother had visited the surgery on 25 September and he had told her that Mary had gone to Edinburgh with Mrs Ruxton, who was caring for Mary after she had had a pregnancy terminated. The story just didn't ring true, and Mrs Rogerson told Ruxton that if Mary wasn't home by the weekend she would go to the police.

Dr Ruxton was well known to Lancaster police; more than once he had been reported by his wife for assault, and when detectives decided to pay him a visit he confirmed his wife and maid had gone away following Mary's abortion.

Ruxton's real name was Bukhtyar Rustomji Ratnji Hakim, a Parsee, born to respectable, well-to-do parents in Bombay in 1899. He had graduated from Bombay University as a Bachelor of Medicine and a Bachelor of Surgery. After a short time as a ship's doctor, he returned to Bombay Medical College and received a scholarship at London University College Hospital, and after working in several European cities he settled in Edinburgh, where he met an attractive divorcee, Isabella Van Ess, who since the separation from her Dutch husband was working as a manageress in a city-centre restaurant. Ruxton, a neurotic, volatile young man, seemed to have found his equal in Isabella, and after a stormy courtship they moved in together as man and wife.

In the spring of 1930, Ruxton, now the doting father of a baby daughter, moved his family to Lancaster, taking over a doctor's surgery at 2 Dalton Square. He became well respected and his family increased with the birth of another daughter. They employed a young housekeeper, Mary Jane Rogerson, to look after the children. Her presence seemed to diffuse the tension in the house for a time, but by early 1934 Ruxton was frequently resorting to violence against his wife. Although he was quick to beg her forgiveness when he calmed down, on more than one occasion she had reported him to the police after he had made threats to kill her.

Detectives followed up Mrs Rogerson's claims and found there was nothing unduly suspicious in Ruxton's statement and, satisfied for the time being that the doctor was telling the truth, they left. Enquires showed that Isabella had visited her sister in Blackpool on 14 September, and this was the last time she was seen alive.

Meanwhile, the investigation continued in Scotland. As Professor Glaister and his team worked on identifying the bodies, detectives concentrated on the newspapers that the limbs were wrapped up in: they were found to come from an edition of the *Sunday Graphic*, a nationally distributed newspaper, but the pages that contained the limbs revealed a massive clue. One of the sheets contained the heading '----AMBE'S CARNIVAL QUEEN CROWNED.' Dated 15 September 1935, the heading came from a special 'slip edition' of the *Sunday Graphic* only available in Morecambe, Lancaster and the immediate area. There would had have been less than 4,000 copies of this edition printed.

The disappearance of Mary Rogerson had appeared in several papers, including the *Daily Record*, a copy of which was read by the Chief Constable of Dumfries – who relayed his suspicions that the disappearance might have something to do with the bodies in the river.

Gardenholme Linn, Moffattshire. (Author's Collection)

Isabella Van Ess (left) and Dr Buck Ruxton (right). (Both Author's Collection)

Things now moved at a pace. Detectives re-interviewed Ruxton, while others questioned members of his staff and neighbours. Again they couldn't find anything suspicious, and two days later Ruxton stormed into Lancaster police station and demanded to speak to Captain Henry Vann, the Chief Constable.

'Can't you publish it in the papers that there is no connection between the bodies found in Scotland and the disappearance of my wife?' He pleaded. Captain Vann said that if and when he was satisfied that Ruxton wasn't involved he would consider his request.

Detectives checking items of clothing found in the stream had at last found conclusive proof linking them to the missing women. One item, a blouse, had been repaired with a makeshift patch and Mrs Rogerson confirmed that the repair was her own handiwork, even showing officers the material from which the patch had been cut. Ruxton was asked to return to the station and make another statement and the following morning, 14 October, he was charged with the murder of his wife and housemaid.

Officers converged on Ruxton's house and examined it in minute detail. There was an odd yellow sheen on the bath, which a pathologist confirmed was dried blood. It appeared that the dissection of the bodies had taken place in the bath, and further examinations – which found blood under the adjacent floorboards – confirmed this.

When Ruxton stood trial at Manchester Assizes before Mr Justice Singleton in March 1936, he had in his corner a formidable counsel led by the great Norman Birkett. Ruxton was to be the only witness called by the defence, and when he took his place in the dock he made a pitiful showing. Frequently in tears, he strenuously denied all charges and in replying to the charge that he murdered his housemaid he replied, 'It is absolute bunkum with a capital B, if I may say so. Why should I kill young Mary?' The prosecution suggested that he had killed Mary after she had stumbled in on him after he had murdered his wife.

The eleven-day trial ended when the all-male jury took just one hour to find him guilty. Ruxton appealed against the verdict, but the appeal was quickly dismissed.

On Tuesday 12 May he was hanged at Strangeways and the following Sunday a remarkable note confessing the murder appeared in the *News of the World*:

Lancaster
14.10.35
I killed Mrs Ruxton in a fit of temper because I thought she had been with a man. I was mad at the time. Mary Rogerson was present at the time.
I had to kill her.
B. Ruxton

Warders post a notice of Buck Ruxton's execution on the prison gates, May 1936. (Author's Collection)

The confession was dated on the day of his arrest and had been given to a journalist for a fee of £3,000, money used to pay his defence costs, and which allowed him to engage the most eminent defence counsel of the day. It had been in a sealed envelope only to be opened after Ruxton's death.

78

MAXIE THE DWARF

Max Mayer Haslam, 4 February 1937

Max Mayer Haslam was not the sort of person to blend into a crowd. Bow-legged and standing at a little over 4ft 6in tall, at 23-years-old he was known in the pubs and boarding houses of Nelson as 'Maxie the dwarf'. On Monday 22 June 1936, a man walked into Nelson police station and said that a dwarf was hawking jewellery around the local pubs. He said the goods were high quality and almost certainly stolen, and Maxie had said he had killed a dog while obtaining the jewellery.

Detectives visited a number of pawnshops and soon gathered up a number of objects recently sold by a dwarf, items which he clearly did not appreciate the true value of. One jeweller told police he recognised selling one item of the recovered jewellery to 70-year-old spinster Ruth Clarkson. Ruth lived at 56 Clayton Street, Nelson, sharing her tiny terrace house with her pet fox terrier, Roy.

Although outwardly living a life of poverty, with a house that fitted perfectly with the picture of 1930s depression, one or two locals knew that all was not as it appeared at Clayton Street. Despite her appearance and squalid existence, Ms Clarkson was a wealthy woman owning a number of houses in the town, as well as a large amount of expensive Victorian jewellery.

Detectives called at the house on Clayton Street. Speaking to the neighbours, they discovered no one had seen her or heard the dog barking for several days. They entered the house to be greeted by a horrific sight. The house was in a dreadful state: empty food tins, old newspapers and dirty bottles and plates were everywhere. Mice scurried across the floor, gnawing at scraps of food left on the kitchen table.

Lying on the floor was the battered body of Ruth Clarkson. She had numerous gashes on her head and upper body caused by the bloodstained tyre lever that lay beside the body. There was blood everywhere – pools on the floor and streaks along the walls and ceiling. But the horror didn't end there. Upstairs in the bedroom, the pet dog was bloodied and battered and suspended from the metal headboard.

Haslam was arrested within the hour. He denied any knowledge of the murder of Miss Clarkson, and although he was still in possession of a number of items of her jewellery, he simply claimed they were his own property.

He pleaded not guilty when he stood trial at Manchester Assizes before Mr Justice Lawrence on 8 December 1936. The court heard that Haslam had been born in Heywood just before the First World War into a large family. He had a crippling bone disease that left him unable to walk until he was nine, and by the time he reached his twenties his growth had been stunted and he was severely bow-legged. The disability caused him to become a surly loner and he struggled at school.

When he was made redundant from his job in a cotton mill in the economic decline of the mid-1930s, he turned to a life of crime. After a number of convictions and prison terms for bungled robberies, he was released from Strangeways just a month before he was arrested for murder.

On his release, Haslam returned to Nelson, where he moved into lodgings on Vernon Street. He became friendly with two unemployed labourers and the three men spent their days moping around the town centre on the look out for – and plotting ways to make – some quick money. He then learned about the supposed wealth of Ruth Clarkson, and although the three men usually discussed planned jobs, Haslam wanted to keep the spoils of this one, and carried it out alone.

His defence was that his two 'friends' were responsible for the crime and they had concocted an alibi for the purpose of framing their former friend.

Police sketch made at 56 Clayton Street.
(Author's Collection)

Maxie the Dwarf. (Author's Collection)

Ruth Clarkson's home in Nelson.
(Author's Collection)

*Amid the squalor inside the
house lay the body of Ruth
Clarkson. Her hand can be
made out in the centre of the
photograph.* (TNA:PRO)

The prosecution called a witness who testified he had sold the tyre lever found at the scene of the crime to Haslam two days before the murder. Another witness saw Haslam drop an item down a drain on Leeds Road. Police lifted the grid and discovered a watchcase which had once belonged to Miss Clarkson.

In the face of a wealth of evidence, including Haslam's weak alibi that he was at a cricket match when the crime was committed, the three-day trial ended in the only possible verdict; the jury deliberated for just less than an hour. His appeal in January was dismissed and he was returned to Strangeways to await execution.

Haslam was due to be hanged alongside George Royle, a Stockport man who had killed a woman in the 'East Lancs Road Murder', but just hours before the scheduled double execution Royle was reprieved. Haslam's brother waited outside the prison in tears for notice of execution to be posted, telling a reporter that his father had refused to see Haslam while awaiting execution. In fact, he had said that if the authorities hadn't have hanged him he would have strung him up himself!

79

THE BOYFRIEND

Horace William Brunt, 12 August 1937

One Saturday afternoon, 24 April 1937, while her husband Hugo and daughter Elsie had gone to market to sell eggs, 54-year-old farmer's wife Kate Collier was shot dead in her farmhouse at Bradley, Ashbourne, Derbyshire. When they returned home they discovered her body lying on the kitchen floor. She had been shot in the back of her neck.

The murder weapon was found to be Collier's own shotgun, which the killer had taken down from its place above the kitchen door; after use, it had been replaced. Collier told police that the gun had been used as it had been replaced the wrong way round, and on closer examination it was found that an empty cartridge remained inside the gun.

When officers asked Hugo if he could think of anyone who might be responsible for the murder, the first name to spring to mind was 32-year-old Horace Brunt, Elsie's boyfriend of five years. Brunt was a regular visitor at the farm, but both her parents, and in particular Mrs Collier, did not approve of him and had told him so on a number of occasions. The previous afternoon Hugo and Kate were working on the farm building a chicken pen when Brunt called. He tried to make conversation with Mrs Collier but she was dismissive and told him that if he had come to see Elsie then he should go and find her.

Brunt was interviewed by detectives and initially denied any involvement in the shooting. A witness came forward to say they had seen him cycling up to the farm earlier, on the afternoon she was murdered, and when re-interviewed Brunt made a further statement admitting that he had gone to the farm to try to reconcile any differences Mrs Collier may have had with him.

The Colliers' farmhouse at Ashbourne, Derbyshire. (T.J. Leech Archive)

However, when he arrived she took down the shotgun and began threatening him with it. He claimed they had a brief struggle during which the gun went off accidentally.

At his trial before Mr Justice Singleton at Derby on 2 July, Brunt maintained that the death was accidental. Asked why he had failed to get medical assistance if this was the case, he said he panicked and was scared because he felt certain no one would believe him.

The prosecution put forward a strong case of premeditated murder. They alleged that Kate Collier had recently told her daughter's boyfriend that she would never give her blessing to their relationship and she wished Elsie would find someone else. A gunsmith examined the murder weapon and gave evidence that it was impossible for it to be fired by accident. Crucially, it was found that the murder weapon must have been fired from a distance of at least 6ft, which ruled out any chance of an accidental discharge during a struggle.

Also telling was the type of cartridge found in the gun. This was a different brand to those used by Collier, but a number of this type of cartridge were found at Brunt's home in nearby Upper Mayfield. This suggested the killer had taken the cartridges with him to use in the gun, which he knew was kept at the house.

Brunt was of a low intelligence, but there was no evidence he was insane, and he was duly convicted. His appeal was likewise rejected and with executions no longer carried out at Derby he was sent to Manchester and an 8 a.m. appointment with hangman Tom Pierrepoint.

80

DEATH WISH

Charles James Caldwell, 20 April 1938

Charlie Caldwell had met his Swiss-born wife Eliza while he was interned during the First World War. Although he was almost ten years older they soon fell in love, and following the Armistice they married and moved to his hometown of Rochdale, where he found work in the local cotton mills and she brought up their two children.

By the turn of 1938, relations between 49-year-old Caldwell and his wife had deteriorated. The depression that hit the north of England in the 1930s meant that Caldwell found himself out of work, although with the children grown up Eliza was able to find a job as a seamstress. He took to working as a hawker but money was scarce and they were constantly arguing about their finances and the fact that Eliza refused to give her husband any of her wages to spend on drink. This caused numerous arguments, and after tolerating this for long enough she told him she wanted a separation, packed her bags and moved out.

Although Caldwell pleaded with her to come back to him, Eliza had decided the split was to be final and took steps to make it official. On 7 February she saw a solicitor and took out a summons against her husband on account of wilfully neglecting to maintain her, cruelty and desertion. Over the next few days he made several attempts to get her to return home to him, each time without success. Eliza told him bluntly she was not interested in any form of reconciliation.

On Friday evening, 11 February, Caldwell waited for Eliza to finish work and waylaid her as she made her way home down Halifax Road. He asked her one more time to return to him: when she curtly dismissed him, he pulled out a large knife and stabbed her once in the chest. Bleeding profusely, Eliza staggered into a nearby butcher's shop where she collapsed onto the floor and died before medical assistance could be given.

Caldwell was soon arrested. When taken into custody he made a failed attempt to cut his throat with a small knife he had concealed in his boot. As charges were explained to him he burst into tears and exclaimed, 'She is gone ... I want the rope now.'

Woman Fatally Stabbed

LAST NIGHT'S HEYBROOK TRAGEDY

VICTIM'S HUSBAND ARRESTED

SPECIAL COURT TO-DAY

At about six o'clock last night a woman was fatally stabbed outside the butcher's shop, 27 Halifax Road, Hamer. She had received a severe wound on the left side of the chest just above the region of the heart, and after calling out something she collapsed and died almost immediately. Her assailant ran away before anyone in the vicinity could stop him, though the blow was witnessed, it is stated, by a customer.

The police were immediately informed and within a short time the victim was identified as

Elisa Augustine Caldwell, aged 44 years, of 27 Clementina Street, Rochdale.

Above: *The murder of Eliza Caldwell made headlines across the country.* (Author's Collection)

Right: *Eliza Caldwell.* (Author's Collection)

His trial before Mr Justice Tucker on 14 March was a formality. He offered a defence of insanity but the prosecution's case, that he stabbed his wife in a jealous rage, was enough for the jury to return a guilty verdict. Caldwell refused to appeal against conviction, claiming that he wished to die. A month later he got his wish.

81

THE SEPARATION ORDER

Clifford Holmes, 11 February 1941

When news reached 24-year-old Clifford Holmes, a driver in the Royal Engineers based at Gibraltar Barracks, Aldershot, that the summons his wife had taken out against him was due to be heard in a Manchester court, he asked for, and was granted, short notice leave.

Clifford and Irene Holmes had married in 1935 and had two young children, but there had been problems in the relationship and the family was under the care of a Probation Officer. In January 1940 Holmes wrote a letter to his wife, which he illustrated with rude drawings and filled with a number of sexual references. Irene had told the officer that since the birth of the youngest child Holmes had subjected her to what she termed indecent practices.

The officer wrote to Holmes and warned him to modify his behaviour, and when Holmes returned home on leave in the summer, husband and wife seemed to be on good terms. It was following a

Feb. 11. 1941.

Name   Clifford Holmes.

Height.   5 - 6½ ins.

Age   24 years - Weight 136 lbs.

Drop   8'- 1 ins.

Remarks,

Very good job carried out
at Strangeways by
Mr Thomas W. Pierrepoint
Very cheerfull

Time taken 14 seconds

*Clifford Holmes'
execution as recorded in
assistant hangman Harry
Allen's diary. (Author's
Collection)*

visit at the end of August that Irene claimed Holmes had threatened her with his rifle and bayonet, and as a result she took out the summons against him.

On 5 October Holmes returned to Manchester and tried in vain to get her to withdraw the summons: three days later they appeared in court, where Irene was granted the separation order on the grounds of his persistent cruelty. As they left the courtroom Holmes shouted at her, 'You won't get a penny out of me, I'll do you in first!' Fearing for her safety Irene and the children moved out of the family home and took rooms in nearby Longsight.

On Thursday 10 October, Holmes tracked her down to a flat on 450 Stockport Road, and after spending the afternoon drinking he called at the house. One of the tenants, Florence Farrington, heard him knocking on the front door at just before 8.30 p.m., and when she opened the door Holmes burst past her and headed for the stairs, shouting for Irene to open her door.

When she refused Holmes raised the rifle and blasted the lock. As Mrs Farrington rushed to get help Holmes discharged his rifle again: the bullet thudded into the wall, and as he reloaded Irene tried to escape by rushing down the stairs. Finding herself cornered in the kitchen, however, she begged him to have mercy – instead, Holmes shot her once in the breast before stabbing her four times with the bayonet as she slumped to the floor. It was then claimed that Holmes began to sexually assault his wife before he was restrained by a police officer. He then made an attempt to shoot himself, but finally he handed over the gun, claiming he lacked the courage to do it himself.

Insanity was to be his defence at his trial before Mr Justice Stable in December. Evidence was heard that Holmes was sexually obsessed to the point of insanity and the evidence of the sexual assault on his wife's murdered body supported this. They also told the court that Holmes' brother was a certified mental defective.

The prosecution claimed it was simply another case of a spurned husband enraged because his wife had taken out the separation order against him. They pointed to the threats he had made after leaving the courtroom and they also suggested that Holmes may have killed Irene because he believed she had been unfaithful to him.

82

THE FIFTH BULLET

John Smith, 4 September 1941

The meeting at Whitworth Salvation Hall on Sunday afternoon, 18 May 1941, had been well attended, but one member of the audience couldn't wait for it to end. Twenty-eight-year-old Margaret 'Ellen' Knight had just taken her seat, when someone slid into the seat behind her whose presence she was very unhappy about.

John Smith was a 32-year-old cotton worker serving in the newly formed Home Guard, and, sporting the uniform and carrying his rifle, he took the pew behind her and smiled when she noticed his presence.

Smith had been keeping company with Ellen for over four months, and when she announced she was pregnant, Smith, of Shawford, near Rochdale, was delighted at the news and proposed marriage. Ellen, however, had come to realise that the relationship was going nowhere and was aghast. 'I'd rather die than marry him,' she told her mother when she learned of Smith's proposal. Ellen had then broken off their relationship and made plans to terminate her pregnancy, and had gone to great lengths to avoid contact with Smith.

When the meeting ended Ellen and her two friends, Alice Shorrocks and Doris Crossley, quickly made for the door and set off down Market Street. Smith soon fell in behind them and they had only gone a few paces when Doris remembered she needed to pass a message to a friend and returned inside. Ellen and Alice set off down the road followed by Smith. Doris had passed on her message and just exited the hall to rejoin her friends when she saw Smith raise his rifle, point it at Ellen and squeeze the trigger. One shot rang out and Ellen slumped to the ground.

As people rushed to her aid – and someone called the police – Smith stood stunned, mumbling it was an accident over and over again. Ellen died from her wounds before the ambulance arrived.

At his trial before Mr Justice Hallett on 8 July, the background to the sorry tale was told to the court. Although Smith had made an attempt to flee the scene once he had come to his senses, he was told to stop by the policeman who had been called to the scene. He meekly handed over his weapon, claiming that he didn't know it was loaded and that he had only meant to frighten her into changing her mind about ending their relationship.

Smith's main defence witness was his drill sergeant with the Home Guard, who testified that the accused was the worst shot he had ever seen and that he could not even aim straight. He also said that none of the men in his platoon knew how to handle a rifle and it was quite believable that Smith may not have been aware if the rifle was loaded or not.

On the day before the murder the men had been on parade and had later been issued with a clip containing five rounds of ammunition. When this was returned to the stores, Smith's clip contained just four rounds. He told the quartermaster he could not find the fifth bullet. The drill sergeant told the court it was quite possible that the bullet was in the rifle without Smith knowing this.

Smith may have got away with a manslaughter charge had he not changed his story under cross-examination and admitted that he slipped the fifth bullet in the rifle shortly before he visited the hall that Sunday afternoon, though his intention had only been to fire over her head and frighten Ellen.

The jury, finding Smith guilty of murder, added a strong recommendation for mercy. Smith launched an appeal but on being consulted the trial judge told the appeal court that he believed it was a premeditated murder and all the evidence supported this.

Ellen Knight lies dead in the street. (TNA:PRO)

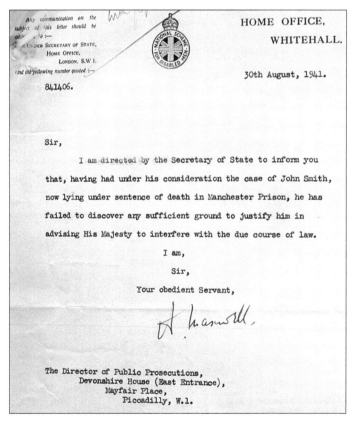

No reprieve for John Smith. (Author's Collection)

83

THE LOCKED CABIN

James Galbraith, 26 July 1944

After a perilous voyage across the Atlantic the merchant vessel *Pacific Shipper* made its way slowly up the River Mersey to its mooring at Salford's No. 9 dock. A week later, on Saturday 8 April 1944, the body of 48-year-old wireless operator James William Percey was found in his locked cabin. It was a clear case of murder: he had been battered to death with an axe and robbed of his recently collected pay packet. In the cabin were several empty bottles of beer along with two tumblers, one containing a set of fingerprints believed to be those of the killer, who was presumably the man in whose company Percey was seen returning to the ship the last time he was seen alive.

Detectives began to piece together his movements leading up to the murder. Percey was a native of Montreal, Canada, and shortly after arriving in Salford he had travelled to Liverpool to collect his wages plus some extra money owed as compensation for property lost when his ship had been torpedoed. In total he collected £87 with some of the notes from a new batch, consecutively numbered from A 88 E 514001 to 514500. The missing money suggested a clear motive for the murder.

They also quickly had a prime suspect. A cargo worker at the docks told detectives he had seen a man accompany Percey onto the ship and recognised him as James Galbraith, a 26-year-old Merchant Navy steward who lived with his mother on Moss Road, Stretford. Galbraith was a habitual criminal and known to be short of money, having had to borrow money from a friend shortly before the murder. In the last few days, detectives learned, Galbraith had purchased a new coat for £7 and given his mother money for his keep.

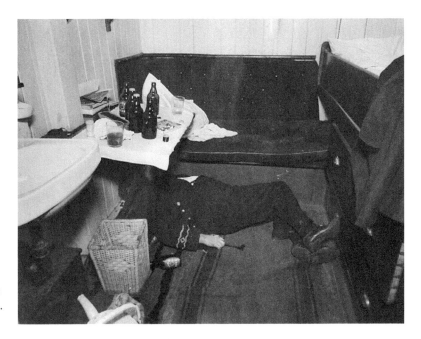

The body of James Percey in his cabin. (TNA:PRO)

Police scene of crime photo showing the entrance to the cabins on the Pacific Shipper. (TNA:PRO)

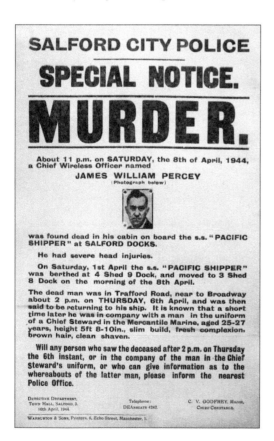

SALFORD CITY POLICE

SPECIAL NOTICE.

MURDER.

About 11 p.m. on SATURDAY, the 8th of April, 1944, a Chief Wireless Officer named

JAMES WILLIAM PERCEY
(Photograph below)

was found dead in his cabin on board the s.s. "PACIFIC SHIPPER" at SALFORD DOCKS.

He had severe head injuries.

On Saturday, 1st April the s.s. "PACIFIC SHIPPER" was berthed at 4 Shed 9 Dock, and moved to 3 Shed 8 Dock on the morning of the 8th April.

The dead man was in Trafford Road, near to Broadway about 2 p.m. on THURSDAY, 6th April, and was then said to be returning to his ship. It is known that a short time later he was in company with a man in the uniform of a Chief Steward in the Mercantile Marine, aged 25-27 years, height 5ft 8-10in., slim build, fresh complexion, brown hair, clean shaven.

Will any person who saw the deceased after 2 p.m. on Thursday the 6th instant, or in the company of the man in the Chief Steward's uniform, or who can give information as to the whereabouts of the latter man, please inform the nearest Police Office.

DETECTIVE DEPARTMENT,
TOWN HALL, SALFORD, 3.
10th April, 1944.

Telephone:
DEANSGATE 4242.

C. V. GODFREY, MAJOR,
CHIEF CONSTABLE.

WARBURTON & SONS, Printers, 6, Echo Street, Manchester, 1.

Left: *Wanted notice issued during the hunt for Percey's killer.* (Author's Collection)

Below: *Galbraith's weight and youth meant he received one of the longest drops given in modern times.* (Author's Collection)

Fortunately his mother still had one of the notes and it was found to be one of those issued to Percey. While this note alone would not be enough, officers traced Galbraith's spending and managed to trace a total of forty notes from the batch issued to the murdered sailor.

Arrested three days later, Galbraith admitted he had been with Percey in the cabin and claimed they had gone there for more drinks after last orders. He said he had stayed for over an hour, but although he admitting stealing the money from a drawer when Percey went to the bathroom, he was adamant the man was alive and well when he departed. However, a search of his room found clothes with traces of blood on them which matched the blood type of the murdered man

Faced with a wealth of evidence against him Galbraith was charged with murder and his trial took place before Mr Justice Hilbery at the end of May. Asked to explain how Percey's blood appeared on his clothes, Galbraith said that the Canadian had asked Galbraith to help him shave while they were in the cabin, and he had accidentally nicked him with the razor; this was easily disproved as the dead man's chin was covered with stubble. On the third day of his trial the jury took just a short time to find Galbraith guilty as charged.

Galbraith was a slight man standing 5ft 5in and weighing just 123lbs, and as a result hangman Tom Pierrepoint gave him a drop of 8ft 11in, one of the longest drops recorded in modern times.

84

HANGED FOR A DIRTY WEEKEND

Harold Berry, 9 April 1946

The black Ford Eight slowly coasted to a halt and the farmer watched as the driver looked around before walking quickly up the dirt track beside Moulton Hall Farm, Winsford, and disappearing into the night. It was Thursday evening, 3 January 1946. The following morning the car was still there, and police soon traced it to the Refuge Lending Society in Manchester. Staff there said it was the company car of their managing clerk, 37-year-old Bernard Phillips, whose wife Kitty had reported him missing when he had failed to return to their home in Prestwich, Manchester, the previous evening.

Two days later two young brothers discovered the body of a man in a culvert close to the farm where the car was dumped. Home Office pathologist Dr Walter Grace told detectives that the victim had died from a stab wound to the left shoulder, which had punctured his lung. A commando bayonet recovered from beside the body was soon traced to one Harold Berry, a 30-year-old father of four who worked as a watchman at Winsford's CWS bacon factory. Detectives called at his house and found that he wasn't at home; his wife told the officers that he was in London with the wife of a soldier he had been carrying on with. Detectives learned Berry was due back on Monday and planned to visit a friend at Pendleton, Salford, where he was arrested that night.

On Valentine's Day 1946, Berry found himself before Mr Justice Stable at Cheshire Assizes. He pleaded not guilty and the court heard of the events that led to the death of Bernard Phillips. Berry had met 21-year-old Irene Wynne, the pretty wife of a soldier serving overseas, in the previous autumn when she started work at the same factory where Berry worked. They soon began an affair and would meet up several nights a week, often drinking in the pubs and clubs around Northwich.

With her husband serving overseas, Irene had returned to live with her mother, and with Berry having a wife and four children at home, their courting was limited to furtive kissing in mostly public places. He decided to plan a romantic weekend in London's West End and when he told Irene she agreed at once.

Cheshire murderer Harold Berry. (Author's Collection)

This presented Berry with a problem. His meagre wages from the bacon factory were barely enough to support his wife and family, let alone pay for three nights of passion in London. At 11 a.m. on 3 January, Berry had called into offices of the Refuge Lending Society, seeking a loan of £50. He gave his name as George Wood, poultry farmer, of Tarporley, Cheshire.

Phillips told the customer he would have to visit the address in person before he could authorise the release of the loan. Phillips told him he would arrange to call on Sunday afternoon, as it would be a nice drive out for him and his wife. 'Mr Wood's' stressed the loan was urgent and they arranged to meet that afternoon. At 2 p.m., Berry and the manager, with a suitcase containing the money, set out in the black Ford Eight.

The prosecution called a witness who testified that he had sold Berry the commando knife for 10s shortly before Christmas 1945 and a cashier at the Refuge Lending Society identified Berry as the man who had signed the paperwork as George Wood, and who had left the office in the company of Mr Phillips. The missing money was also traced to London; as was the practice at the time, Berry's signature was on the back of the £5 notes.

Irene Wynne told the court of the trip to London and how Berry had showered her with expensive gifts and extravagant luxuries. She told how they had stayed in rooms costing £1 per night, when Berry's income was barely £5 a week. He spent money on theatre and cinema tickets, bought two books costing 20s, and drinks in a number of bars and public houses. In total, Berry had spent over £20 in London.

Berry denied the charge against him and blamed a man named Greenwood for the murder, but his alibi could not be substantiated and the evidence against him was too strong.

It took the jury less than an hour to find Berry guilty as charged and he was sentenced to death. Perhaps Berry counted the cost of his trip to London as he awaited the hangman: the lives of two young men, the widowing of two women and four young children left without a father. That was the true cost of Harold Berry and Irene Wynne's 'dirty weekend'.

85

A SOUVENIR FROM THE WAR

Martin Patrick Coffey, 24 April 1946

Sitting in the lounge at the Salvation Hostel, Martin Coffey picked up the newspaper and boasted to his friends, as he read the report of the shooting, that he had committed the crime.

The previous day, Monday 26 November 1945, the 24-year-old Irish-born habitual criminal had entered a pawnshop at 57 Great Jackson Street, Hulme, and, pointing a gun at the proprietor, 72-year-old Henry Dutton, demanded all the money in the shop. Dutton reluctantly unlocked the safe, which contained over £2,000, but as Coffey reached for the money, the old man blew a police whistle. Coffey fired the gun, hitting him in the thigh. Undeterred, Dutton continued to blow on the whistle, and in a panic Coffey shot him twice in the chest before fleeing without the money. As Coffey made his getaway, Dutton followed him out of the door before collapsing in the street.

Coffey bragged about the shooting to a number of lodgers at the hostel, including his closest friend Johnny Irvine, and one of the lodgers soon informed the police. Although gravely ill, Dutton made a statement from his hospital bed and described the gunman as around 5ft 7in tall, clean shaven, in his early twenties and wearing a trilby hat.

When Coffey was questioned about his movements on the day of the shooting his answers were vague and his movements unsubstantiated. Although he did fit the description of the assailant, a search of his room failed to locate any bloodstained clothing or anything else linking him to the crime. Nevertheless he was taken into custody under suspicion of attempted murder.

A further search was ordered of the hostel and in Irvine's room, hidden on top of a cupboard, they found the murder weapon. Irvine said that he had been offered the gun, which was 'a souvenir from the war', by Coffey. With the gun located, Coffey made a further statement admitting that he was responsible for the shooting, but claimed that it had been accidental.

Henry Dutton's pawn shop. (TNA:PRO)

Martin Patrick Coffey (right) was the last man hanged at Manchester by long-standing hangman Thomas Pierrepoint (above). (Author's Collection)

Four days later Dutton died from his injuries and Coffey was charged with wilful murder. When he appeared before Mr Justice Morris at Manchester Assizes on 13 March, Coffey's defence counsel claimed that the prisoner was a fantasist who had boasted about and confessed to the murder to give him some 'kudos' among his fellow lodgers.

The prosecution claimed it was wilful murder committed following a botched robbery, as Coffey matched the description given by the dead shopkeeper and a number of witnesses who saw a man fleeing the scene of the crime. The murder weapon was also traced to Coffey; he had purchased the gun as a souvenir from a Canadian soldier.

His execution marked the last visit to the prison by aged hangman Tom Pierrepoint, who had made his first visit to Strangeways thirty-seven years before. It was also the last execution carried out by Manchester-born assistant hangman Alex Riley, who lived just a few streets from where the murder took place, and who had become a hangman just before the outbreak of the war.

86

'BECAUSE OF MY PAST'

Walter Graham Rowland, 27 February 1947

'It will suit my purposes,' the man told the shopkeeper, handing over the 3s 6d for the flat-faced leather-maker's hammer. Placing it into his raincoat pocket he left the shop in the Manchester suburb of Ardwick and headed off towards the city centre.

On Sunday morning, 20 October 1946, two young boys playing on a bombsite on the corner of Deansgate and Cumbernauld Street discovered the body of a woman. A search of the area yielded three clues: a bloodstained, flat-faced hammer; some wrapping paper, shaped as if it had been around a hammer, and a card that revealed the woman's identity as Olive Balchin, a known prostitute.

Several witnesses were able to give police a description of the man seen rowing with a woman in the area on the Saturday night: all agreed the man had dark hair and a fresh complexion and was dressed in a dark suit and light raincoat.

As detectives combed the city looking for clues, a resident at the Services' Transit dormitory reported that a man named Roland had taken his raincoat and failed to return it. As the witnesses had mentioned the man police were seeking was wearing a light raincoat, a detective was sent to investigate and found that Roland was actually Walter Graham Rowland, a man with a long string of convictions dating back to the 1920s, and who in 1934 had been convicted of murder. Rowland was also found to have been a regular client of the murdered woman.

Questioned about the murder case, Rowland admitted knowing Olive Balchin and suggested a possible motive when he told detectives he was being treated for venereal disease, which he believed he had caught from Olive Balchin.

Although all leads so far led to Rowland, he seemed to have an alibi for the night of the murder, which, he claimed, could be substantiated by police in Stockport who had visited a pub where Rowland claimed he was in for most of the night. Rowland said that, after leaving the pub, he caught a bus back to Manchester, booking in to a lodging house at 81 Brunswick Street. The landlord of the lodging house confirmed the alibi. However, an identity parade was held and Rowland was picked out by all the witnesses who claimed to have seen the couple arguing on the night of the murder.

Charged with the wilful murder of Olive Balchin, Rowland stood trial before Mr Justice Sellers at Manchester Assizes in mid-December. His defence was based around an alibi for the Saturday night, but this was found to have many gaps in it, mainly relating to the lodging house where he claimed to have stayed in Ardwick. Rowland claimed he had signed in on the Saturday night, but a check of the register found he had stayed there on the Friday.

Rowland was also identified as the man who had purchased the hammer, and forensic evidence found traces of dirt identical to that on the bombsite in the turn up on Rowland's trousers. The trial lasted four days and it took the jury less than two hours to find Rowland guilty of murder – and so, for the second time in his life, he stood in the dock and heard the judge pass sentence of death on him.

The jury was then informed that in 1934 Rowland had been sentenced to death for the murder of his young daughter. He was scheduled to hang at Strangeways on 14 June 1934, but just forty-eight hours before he was due to hang, Rowland was reprieved. He served eight years imprisonment before being released in June 1942 on condition he joined the armed forces. At Strangeways, Rowland occupied the same cell he had vacated twelve years before. He launched an appeal and a hearing was set for 27 January 1947.

Then, five days before the court hearing, there was a sensational development when the Governor of Walton Gaol, Liverpool, received a note from one of his prisoners. David Ware was serving a short sentence after confessing to a theft from a Salvation Army hostel in Stoke. Ware told the Governor that it was he who had committed the murder of Olive Balchin at Manchester and that Rowland was not guilty.

When Rowland's appeal took place they asked for the verdict to be quashed based on the testimony of Ware. After considering the request in light of the new information received, an application for an adjournment for fourteen days was granted. On 10 February, Rowland's appeal took place at the Central Criminal Court, but the request to hear the evidence of David Ware was refused.

As Lord Goddard dismissed the appeal, Rowland made a passionate speech from the dock: 'I am an innocent man! This is the greatest injustice which has ever happened in an English court. Why did you have the man who confessed here today and not hear him? I am not allowed justice because of my past!'

As Lord Goddard ordered Rowland be taken down he continued his plea: 'It would have knocked the bottom out of English Law to have acquitted me and proved my innocence. I say now I am an innocent man before God.'

Walter Rowland twice occupied the condemned cell at Strangeways.
(Author's Collection)

A week later, with a new date set for the execution, the Home Secretary ordered an inquiry. After analysing all the evidence the panel came to the conclusion that Ware's confession was false, that he had been wrong about the time of the murder and had seemingly just pieced together his confession from newspaper reports.

On 22 February, David Ware withdrew his confession and five days later Rowland was hanged. He left two letters in the condemned cell, written at dawn as he waited to die. The first, to his parents, re-iterated his pleas of innocence; in the other, to his solicitor, Mr Keymer, he wrote that he hoped he would carry on trying to clear his name for a crime he swore he did not commit.

Four years later, David John Ware attempted to murder a woman in Bristol. He had bought himself a new hammer with which to commit the crime. Tried on 16 November 1951, he was found guilty but insane and committed to Broadmoor – where he hanged himself in his cell on 1 April 1954. The case of Walter Graham Rowland has never been reviewed.

87

LIKE A MAN

Margaret Allen, 12 January 1949

'I didn't do it for money... I was in one of my funny moods.'
Statement made by Margaret 'Bill' Allen following her arrest.

Margaret Allen was determined to meet her fate 'like a man'; but as she waited in the condemned cell at Strangeways she seethed in anger at being forced to wear a striped prison frock. On the morning of her execution, with her request to wear men's clothing refused, she kicked over her breakfast and spent her last hours bitter and sullen. She was to be the first woman to be hanged in Great Britain for over twelve years.

Four months before, in the early hours on 29 August 1948, the body of 68-year-old Nancy Chadwick had been discovered lying in Bacup Road, Rawtenstall, outside the house of Margaret Allen. What initially had appeared to be injuries as a result of a hit and run were soon found to have been inflicted by a hammer, and when detectives began their enquiries they soon had a prime suspect in Allen, who seemed to be shadowing officers as they searched for clues in the immediate area.

Margaret Allen was a lesbian who preferred to dress in men's clothing: she would not answer to her own name, but only to 'Bill'. The twentieth of twenty-one children, she had spent several years working as a bus conductress, but following the death of her mother in 1943, she seemed to lose interest in life; she gave up her job and became a loner who took to smoking and drinking heavily.

When officers visited the Allen house they immediately noticed bloodstains on the wall just inside the front doorway, and when they asked her to explain them she made a full confession to the murder. She claimed that she had killed the old woman because she had annoyed her over some trivial incident when she had called at Allen's house. She had then picked up a hammer and struck her several times on the head.

Margaret Allen was charged with murder on her 43rd birthday. When she appeared before Mr Justice Sellars at Manchester Assizes her defence was insanity, which manifested itself in what she called 'funny moods.' The prosecution claimed that after committing the brutal murder Allen had stolen the woman's purse. It was also suggested that the cold way she had described the murder, with lucid and chilling clarity, suggested she was a callous killer rather than someone who was insane.

The jury clearly agreed and took less than fifteen minutes to return their verdict. A petition for a reprieve in her East Lancashire hometown met with little support and from a population of 26,000 just 126 people signed.

Above: *Bloodstains mark the spot where the body of Nancy Chadwick was discovered in the road outside Margaret Allen's home in Rawtenstall.* (Author's Collection)

Right: *Margaret 'Bill' Allen.* (T.J. Leech Archive)

88

TISH

James Henry Corbitt, 28 November 1950

On Saturday night, 19 August 1950, 37-year-old toolmaker and pub tenor James Corbitt spent the evening drinking in a number of pubs in the Ashton-under-Lyne area. One of those that Corbitt and his girlfriend visited that night was the curiously named Help the Poor Struggler in Failsworth. Here he was guaranteed a warm welcome from the landlord, public hangman Albert Pierrepoint. Corbitt and Pierrepoint often sang together in the crowded pub and referred to each other by the friendly names Tish and Tosh. At shortly before closing time Corbitt made for the exit and Pierrepoint called out, 'Goodnight Tish.' Corbitt replied with a smile and a 'Goodnight Tosh', and his girlfriend waved as they made their way out onto the main road. They would meet just one more time.

The following morning, the body of 36-year-old Eliza Wood was found strangled in a room at the Prince of Wales Hotel in Ashton-under-Lyne. Written in eyebrow pencil on her forehead was the word 'whore'. Corbitt was arrested the following day at his lodgings on Portland Street, Manchester. He claimed that he did not know why he had killed Eliza, but that when she began shouting at him he had grabbed her by the throat. When she collapsed on the bed he had tied a bootlace around her neck 'to finish her off.'

Detectives found a diary in Corbitt's possession in which he recorded his thoughts on what was a fraught relationship. One entry dated 11 March read: 'Date with Liza 8.30 p.m. Waited till 10 p.m. Will not wait again. My intentions are to win her affections and when she cannot do without me I will play my final card!' On 23 July there was an entry that stated, 'Took Liza out tonight. Got her drunk ... Could have finished her ... '

At his trial before Mr Justice Lynskey at Liverpool Assizes on 6 November, Corbitt pleaded insanity. The prosecution made reference to the entries in the diary that showed the murder had been planned and that the murder had been the work of a jealous man, as he believed she was planning to leave him for another man.

His defence also referred to the diary, but claimed it supported their view that he was insane and pointed to entries in which he claimed to have headaches all day and that at times his mind was blank.

When hangman Pierrepoint arrived at Strangeways he was unaware that the man he was to hang was his former customer, but was told by the Governor that the condemned man seemed more afraid of being shunned by Pierrepoint than his impending death.

As Pierrepoint entered his cell on the fateful morning Corbitt looked up and smiled meekly. 'Good morning Tosh,' he said quietly. 'Hello Tish,' the hangman replied, and as the prisoner got to his feet he reassured his former friend: 'Come on old chap.'

89

'IF I DID, I DON'T REMEMBER'

Nicholas Persoulious Crosby, 19 December 1950

After three days of intensive questioning the prisoner in the dock had finally been trapped by his contradictions and lies. Asked again by the prosecution if he had killed the young girl, the accused flustered and admitted, 'To be sure sir, I don't know if I did. If I did, I don't remember.'

On Sunday morning, 9 July 1950, a caretaker checking on his premises at Holbeck, Leeds, discovered the body of Ruth Massey, a 19-year-old seamstress, on spare ground close to the canteen. She was half naked and her throat had been cut.

Medical investigations indicated that she had recently had sex, a used condom found nearby suggesting with her consent, before being violently assaulted and having her throat cut. She had died from the haemorrhaging of the wound.

Detectives learned that Ruth had been seen by her sister in the company of Crosby, a gypsy, as they left a Leeds public house the previous evening. Crosby was picked up for questioning, but claimed he had been so drunk he could not remember anything that had happened after he left the hotel.

His cousin, Gladys Crosby, told police that Crosby had admitted that he had been drinking with Ruth, but that they had been with another man. After leaving the pub the three of them walked towards where Ruth was later found, but Crosby had walked off, leaving the couple alone. He said that moments later he heard a piercing scream – when he rushed back, Ruth was lying dead on the ground. Fearful that the man would also attack him, Crosby had said he would say nothing.

Crosby was charged with murder the following day and tried before Mr Justice Finnemore at Leeds Assizes on 27 November. He denied the charges and gave varying accounts of what had happened: in one, that she had gone off with another man after they had parted; in another, that he had walked her home and that after they had parted – and as he walked away – he heard a scream. He changed his account a number of times and made a poor show in the dock.

His defence was based on the fact that Crosby was drunk when he left the pub and had no recollection of events from then on. They also pleaded insanity, but the jury were not convinced and returned a guilty verdict.

Crosby would normally have been hanged at Leeds, but in line with a modernisation programme at many prisons, the execution suite at Armley Gaol was under construction and Crosby was the first of a number of Yorkshire-based killers sent over the Pennines for execution.

All communications should be
addressed to "The Governor"
and not to any official by name.

H. M. PRISON.

MANCHESTER,

4.12.50,

Dear Sir,

7905. Nicholas Persoulious Crosby.

The above named prisoner is at present in my custody under
sentence of death and the time provisionally fixed for the execution
is Tuesday, the 19th. December, 1950, at 9.0. a.m.

I enclose two copies of a memorandum of conditions for your
perusal, and if you are at liberty to act in the capacity of
Assistant Executioner will you so inform me and sign and return
one copy of the memorandum in the attached envelope, retaining the
other copy for your own reference.

Should you be unable to accept, please return both copies
of the memorandum as soon as possible.

Yours faithfully,

S. Dernley, Esq.,
10, Sherwood Rise,
Mansfield Woodhouse,
Mansfield,
Notts.

Governor.

No. 937   (16676—14-4-26)

Letter inviting hangman Syd Dernley to assist at Crosby's execution. (Author's Collection)

90

THE BODY IN THE HUT

Nenad Kovasevic, 26 January 1951

On Monday morning, 9 October 1950, workmen on the Accrington to Bury railway line discovered the battered body of a man in a trackside hut near Rossendale. He was identified as Radomir Djorovic, a 26-year-old Yugoslavian refugee who lived in Blackburn. Investigations into his movements found that he had last been seen the previous afternoon in the company of another Yugoslav, Nenad Kovasevic, at nearby Edenfield, when other Yugoslavian refugees had invited both men for Sunday dinner.

Detectives went to interview Kovasevic at his lodgings in Blackburn and found that he had fled. They discovered that, earlier that day, he had made enquiries about coach times to London, and this led police to make enquiries at a number of coach companies before stopping a coach at Cannock where Kovasevic was placed under arrest.

At the trial before Mr Justice Jones at Manchester Assizes on 7 December, it was shown that the two men had quarrelled as they made their way across the moors. As the rain began to fall they took shelter in the hut, where they began to talk about the war. Djorovic teased his friend when he began to cry as he told how his family had been killed by the Germans, and to add further insult, he told Kovasevic that he had sided with the Germans. In a rage, Kovasevic picked up an axe that lay on the floor of the hut and struck his friend over the head.

The prosecution suggested that the crime had been deliberate and premeditated, since Kovasevic had stolen Djovoric's watch and wallet and had concealed the traces of blood on him beneath the victim's heavy topcoat. The defence claimed that Kovasevic had simply taken the coat to keep dry from the rain and was unaware of the items – the watch and wallet – in the coat pockets. They also claimed that the intense provocation the accused had suffered was enough for the conviction to be lessened to one of manslaughter.

Killer Nenad Kovasevic went to the gallows kicking and fighting. (T.J. Leech Archive)

The prosecution refuted the evidence of manslaughter by suggesting that as soon as Kovasevic returned to Blackburn he had sold a number of the items taken from the dead man, and any chance the accused may have had of getting the jury to accept a lesser charge, on the grounds of provocation, was lost when it was found that a number of blows had been made to the victim while he was on the floor unable to defend himself.

The jury took just eighty-five minutes to decide that Kovasevic was guilty of a brutal murder and he was sentenced to death. His appeal failed, as did a plea from the exiled King Peter of Yugoslavia, who sent a telegram from Paris, asking for clemency for his countryman. Kovasevic did not go to the gallows without a struggle, having to be dragged kicking and fighting every inch of the way.

91

'THANK GOD IT'S JUST THE ONE!'

James Inglis, 8 May 1951

Alice Morgan seemed to be resting, so the young neighbour, who had popped into her neat terrace house on Cambridge Street, Hull, to see if she needed anything from the shops, slipped quietly out. It was mid-afternoon, Friday 2 February 1951.

The following morning a postman called at the house with a parcel that needed to be signed for. He tried knocking on the door twice during his round, and when he had finished for the morning he went back to try to get the signature he needed. This time he tried the door and shouted inside. There was no answer so he edged inside, gingerly calling out as he entered. As he opened the living room door he could see a figure beneath a blanket on the sofa and when he moved closer to examine what he thought he had saw, he found the body of a woman. She had been strangled and a scarf remained knotted tightly around her neck.

Detectives soon learned that Alice Morgan was a 50-year-old prostitute who worked mainly in the area around Hull docks. They also had a likely suspect: 29-year-old Scotsman James Inglis, whom police officers were already searching for in connection with the attempted murder of his landlady, Amy Gray, the previous evening. Inglis had returned home drunk that Friday afternoon, having walked out of his job at the docks the previous afternoon. His landlady began to question him about how he was going to pay for his board and lodgings if he kept walking out of jobs and in a rage he tried to strangle her. Leaving her unconscious on the floor he then forced the gas meter, stole the few coins inside, and fled.

Inglis was tracked down later that Saturday night and immediately confessed that he had killed Alice Morgan. As he was being cautioned about the murder of Alice, he interrupted and asked if his landlady was also dead. Told she wasn't, he simply replied, 'Thank god it's just the one!'

Inglis said that after he had spent the day drinking with Alice, spending the money he had got from his payoff at the dock on her, he accompanied her to her home. He asked her for sex and she named a price. It was more than Inglis could afford – and besides, he believed that having lavished money on her all afternoon there should not be a charge. When she was adamant she would only sleep with him for the price she quoted he lost his temper and in a rage he attacked her.

Her injuries were appalling: she had been stabbed in the head as well as kicked and punched about the head and upper body before a scarf was fastened so tightly around her neck it needed to be cut away later.

He offered a defence of insanity when he appeared before Mr Justice Gorman at Yorkshire Assizes on 17 April. His grandmother had died in a mental hospital; furthermore, during the war Inglis had been discharged from the army after he was diagnosed as suffering from a psychopathic personality, having also spent three months in a mental hospital. Asked if he had anything to say before sentence was passed, Inglis simply asked that he be hanged as quickly as possible!

They were prophetic words. On the morning of the execution, as assistant Syd Dernley reported later, Inglis was so eager to get to the gallows that he actually began to trot out of the cell, leaving hangman Albert Pierrepoint in his wake. The execution was timed at just seven seconds from the hangmen entering the cell until the brutal killer was hanging dead at the end of the rope.

So eager was James Inglis to get his execution over, he almost ran to the gallows. (Author's Collection)

92

THE MONEYLENDER

John Dand, 12 June 1951

The murder inquiry had begun on Sunday 28 January 1951 when two sisters, who lived either side of 199 Huntington Road, York, the home of 72-year-old widower Walter Wyld, became concerned for their neighbour's health. When he failed to answer the door they entered – and found him stabbed to death on the kitchen floor, his arms bound with flex.

It seemed clear that robbery was the motive; Wyld's trouser pockets had been turned out, and the furniture in the living room was disturbed in such a way as to suggest both signs of a struggle and that someone had been looking for something.

There was no sign of a forced entry, which suggested that the victim had allowed the killer to enter the house. Wyld was a popular and well-known figure in the area. A former rugby league footballer, he had devoted his spare time to his favourite rugby football team, York, and for twenty-five years had served as both gateman and steward at the club. The previous evening he had left York Rugby League social club at 9.45 p.m. and caught the bus alone to Huntington Road, a journey of less than five minutes.

Detectives learned that Wyld often lent out sums of money – anything ranging from a few shillings to several pounds – and letters found in the kitchen drawer led them to Irene Dand, who once lived a few doors away from Wyld in Huntington Road.

In November 1950, the Dand family returned to their native Kirkcaldy, but on 7 January 1951, John Dand returned to York. Thirty-two-year-old Dand was a former soldier with an impressive military record, having been awarded the Military Medal. Interviewed at his lodgings, Dand, in a strong Scots accent, said he had last seen the old man on Monday 8 January, when he paid back a loan.

In Dand's lodgings was a letter from his wife rebuking him for borrowing more money from Wyld after the date Dand had last admitted to seeing the old man, and checks into Dand's statement regarding his movements on the night of the murder found a number of discrepancies; traces of blood on the clothes Dand had submitted for examination matched that of the dead man, and a week after the murder Dand confessed to Scotland Yard detectives that he had killed Wyld following a quarrel over money.

He stood trial before Mr Justice Gorman at Leeds Assizes on 23 April. He denied making the confession to detectives, but the evidence against him was too strong; it took the jury a little over an hour to find him guilty as charged.

Dand chain-smoked on the morning of his execution and even after the hangman had pinioned his arms he asked for a last cigarette.

Military medal holder John Dand. (Author's Collection)

93

NOT ONE FOR SUICIDE

Jack Wright, 3 July 1951

It was 6 a.m. on Sunday 8 April 1951 when two miners finished their shift at Wharton Hall Colliery, Little Hulton, and set out for home. As they made their way across a field they came across a body, lying close to the fence and covered with a raincoat. On closer inspection they saw it was the body of a young woman, with a scarf tied around her neck.

She was identified as Mona Mather, a 28-year-old factory girl. Detectives learned that she had been seen drinking the previous night with members of her family in the George and Dragon pub in Tyldesley. At about 10.30 p.m. she left with a man. They were then seen together heading towards a fair on nearby Shakerley Common.

Within hours of the body being discovered, detectives learned that the man she had left with was a 30-year-old miner from Tyldesley named Jack Wright. Wright and Mona had been courting in the previous year, but had split up when she had left him for another man. Wright called into a local club that afternoon and learned that the police had been looking for him. After finishing his drink he caught a train into Manchester, where he had more to drink and then went to a cinema. Shortly before midnight he was spotted on Manchester's London Road station and taken into custody.

Wright never denied carrying out the crime and made a detailed statement claiming that he had intended to commit a murder: 'I have always had it at the back of my mind to do a job like this.' He said he had planned to kill Mona before they set out for the fair, but as they were walking home in the darkness they stopped by the fence and began kissing. He said she closed her eyes and as she did so he grabbed her throat with his bare hands and strangled her and when she slumped to the ground he finished her off with her own scarf.

Wright pleaded not guilty on account of insanity when he appeared before Mr Justice Oliver at Liverpool Assizes on 12 June. The defence called a psychologist who claimed that Wright had remarked, 'You may think I am stupid, but I believe some evil spirit has taken control of my body. The only thing for me is death. I can do nothing, but I am not one for suicide.' This seemed to imply that by taking a life Wright knew he would forfeit his own. This also suggested he knew what he was doing was wrong and that he would be punished for it.

The same psychologist also told the court that Wright was an aggressive psychopath with a very low intelligence. It was also alleged that Wright had made a number of assaults on females, but in each case the victim had refused to come forward.

Above and right: *Mona Mather's body.* (TNA:PRO)

94

THE NIGHTWATCHMAN MURDER

Alfred Bradley, 15 January 1952

Workers arriving at the Crossacres Estate building site at Wythenshawe, South Manchester, early on the morning of Monday 13 August 1951 were surprised to find the gates were open and Peggy, the watchman's dog, unleashed and roaming free outside. Of the nightwatchman, 58-year-old George Camp, there was no sign.

In recent weeks building sites throughout the area had been the target for thieves who had stolen everything from raw materials to heavy plant machinery. A search of the site ended suddenly when George Camp was found lying in a pool of blood on the floor of the small hut he used for brewing-up. Robbery was initially thought to be the motive.

Detective Chief Supt. Daniel Timpany, head of Manchester CID, arrived to take charge of the investigation. In the hut he discovered a large axe among a pile of wooden planks that had been toppled over. This was initially assumed to be the murder weapon, though the post-mortem was to reveal this was not the case. Camp had indeed died as a result of being beaten to death and the injuries sustained had been pretty horrific: the watchman's chest had been staved in; he had fractured ribs – front and back – and a shattered jaw. The murder weapon, however, wasn't the heavy axe recovered from the murder scene; rather the killer had picked up one of the large blood-stained planks, found beside the body, and used this to beat the old man to death.

Detectives discovered George Camp was a single man, described as an easygoing, friendly chap who never quarrelled with anyone. It was found that on the previous Friday afternoon, a witness had seen George Camp playing cards with a young man in the Red Lion, a public house in nearby Gatley, and again later that night, the witness saw Camp in the same company in the Benchill Hotel.

A description of the man was issued and he was described as aged around 27; stocky build; between 5ft 6ins and 5ft 8ins tall; fresh faced with large hands and wearing a brown suit. Several witnesses gave police similar descriptions of the man seen with George but despite over forty officers being assigned to the investigation, police were unable to match the description to any known criminals and as all leads petered out the trail eventually went cold.

It was to be nearly ten weeks later, on 8 October, before Timpany got the break he had been searching for. It came when the Governor at Strangeways Gaol telephoned the incident room at Northenden, saying he had a man in custody who had confessed to the Wythenshawe murder.

Timpany summoned a car and hurried to the prison, where he spoke to Alfred Bradley, a short, stocky 24-year-old petty thief from Macclesfield, Cheshire, who had been in custody for several days on a minor charge of stealing. Surveying the man Timpany recalled how struck he was by the description on the police wanted notices. Bradley fitted the description on all points.

Bradley admitted that he had murdered the watchman after a quarrel, adding that they had been having a homosexual relationship since the end of the war, when he was aged just seventeen. He said that Camp, who referred to Bradley as Joyce, would pay him for sex, usually £3 or £4 a time.

Asked why he had committed the murder, Bradley said that they had met up in a public house and at Camp's suggestion had gone back to his hut at Wythenshawe. They had quarrelled and during the disagreement Bradley struck the man and killed him. Satisfied the prisoner wasn't wasting his time, Timpany charged him with wilful murder.

On 29 November, Bradley appeared at Manchester Assizes before Mr Justice Lynskey. Called into the dock, he stood facing the judge with one hand in his trouser pocket, clasping the Bible with the

Above: *George Camp's battered body lies on the floor of the hut*. (TNA:PRO) Right: *Killer Alfred Bradley*. (Author's Collection)

other. Veteran defence counsel, Mr Kenneth Burke, defending Bradley, asked him the first question.

'Is your name Alfred Bradley?'

Bradley nodded his reply. The judge looked up at the prisoner and seeing the look of disinterest, snapped, 'Well, is it?'

'Yes,' Bradley muttered.

'Well say so,' he snarled.

Not known for his tolerance, Lynskey cleared his throat and addressed the prisoner.

'Bradley, it is very important from your point of view that those gentlemen on the back row of the jury should hear everything you say, so you will speak so they can do so!'

Still holding the New Testament in his hand, the prisoner suddenly hurled the book at the judge and shouted, 'I have finished with it!'

The book crashed against the bench, showering the judge with water from a tumbler positioned by his side. Bradley was quickly overpowered by warders and carried from the dock shouting and screaming.

Mr Justice Lynskey adjourned the proceedings while Bradley was treated by a doctor in the cells below. Dr George Cormack, the medical officer at Strangeways Gaol, examined the prisoner and found him in a 'highly overwrought state and in no fit state to continue the trial.'

Bradley told the doctor he had no recollection of his behaviour in court. As a result, the trial was postponed to allow Bradley to receive medical attention. A new date was set.

The retrial took place on 7 December. It was held in the same courtroom, but before a new judge and jury. This time Mr Justice Stable presided.

Mr Kenneth Burke again represented Bradley and told the court they were offering a dual defence. Firstly, they said that the death was an accident and that Bradley should be acquitted. Burke said he would show how the two men had quarrelled and that Camp had been injured by falling timber. It would be shown that George Camp had died as a result of being struck by a plank, and although both sides agreed on this point, they differed on how Camp came into contact with it. Burke alleged that it was accidental.

The prosecution countered this by referring to the statement made by Bradley when he was interviewed by the chief inspector at Strangeways in October. Bradley had since denied the statement was true and had blamed the murder on two other men, who he named. His downfall was that he had told too much in his first statement and revealed details only the killer could have known. In his original statement Bradley had described in detail how he had picked up a large plank, weighing almost 50lbs, and battered the old man several times with it.

Burke then offered the defence that Bradley had caused the death of the old man due to severe provocation and that the defendant was only guilty of manslaughter. Burke said that Camp had lured his client, in a drunken state, to the hut and had then committed 'one of the most abominable crimes known to our law.'

It was then alleged Bradley had told Camp he no longer wanted to have any form of relationship with him. The old man had responded by threatening to tell people, and in particular Bradley's parents, that they were lovers, if he carried out his threat. This, the defence counsel pointed out, constituted adequate provocation and as a result, they claimed, Bradley should be tried only on a charge of manslaughter.

The Crown claimed Bradley had gone to the hut willingly enough and performed a sexual act, after which the old man refused to pay Bradley the sum they had agreed. In a fit of rage Bradley then beat the man to death. 'Despite the sordid circumstances,' he went on, 'the facts are that the accused committed a brutal, wilful murder.'

Following Mr Justice Stable's summing up of the case the jury needed less than an hour to return a guilty verdict. Two female members of the jury wept openly as sentence of death was passed.

On the morning he was hanged, the prisoner showed no sign of fear as he awaited the fateful hour, and the Governor later recalled that Bradley had seemed so calm one would have thought he was going to the cinema rather than to his death.

95

IN A FRENZY

Herbert Roy Harris, 26 February 1952

On the evening of Saturday 8 December 1951, the body of a young woman was found on Huntley Bridge, which spans the main Chester to Holyhead railway at Flint, North Wales. Identified as 23-year-old Eileen Harris, a married woman with three young children, who lived on nearby Queen's Avenue with her parents, she had been battered to death with a large stone found beside the body.

Detectives soon issued a statement that they wished to speak to her husband, 24-year-old Herbert Roy Harris, an ex-paratrooper who also lived on Queen's Avenue, though a little farther down, with his own parents, and who had now fled the area.

It seemed a strange domestic arrangement for the mother and children to live in one house and the husband in another, especially as they were still on reasonably good terms. Although they had had to leave their previous lodgings because they were fighting, this new measure was a temporary arrangement as they waited to be allocated a suitable council house.

Eileen had left home at around 5.15 p.m. on Saturday to go to the Plaza cinema. Harris had planned to accompany her but when he called to pick her up he found she had gone without him. He waited for her in a local public house and when she left the cinema they met up and were last seen walking in the direction of Huntley Bridge.

Herbert Roy Harris and his wife, Eileen.
(Author's Collection)

The search for the wanted man was brief. The following day a receptionist at the Regent Palace Hotel, London, was questioned by police asking all hotels and guest houses if the wanted man had booked in, and less than twenty-four hours after the death of his wife, Harris was under arrest.

Harris was returned to North Wales and when charged simply replied that it had not been intentional and that he wished he could turn the clock back.

At his trial before Mr Justice Oliver at Flintshire Assizes, Harris claimed that while they were on the bridge his wife had taunted him that she had deliberately gone to the cinema alone just to annoy him and had then struck him. He claimed he had lost his temper and struck her with the stone, leaving her on the bridge not knowing if she was dead or alive. He had then gone home, changed his clothes and collected his savings before purchasing an overnight train to London. He discovered she was dead when he read it in the paper.

His counsel's plea that the charge be reduced to manslaughter on the grounds of provocation was rejected: the brutal nature of the crime and the prosecution's claims that the fatal blows had been dealt by a man in a frenzy were enough for the jury of ten men and two women to take less than fifty minutes to bring in their verdict. They added a strong recommendation for mercy, which the judge said he would forward to the appropriate quarters. However, Harris chose not to appeal, pinning all his hopes on a reprieve being granted. It was not to be.

96

LOOSE TALK

Louisa May Merrifield, 18 September 1953

The advert for a live-in housekeeper, offering free accommodation for the right person, had resulted in many replies. At 79 years of age, Sarah Ricketts was looking for companionship and someone who could look after the house and see to any odd jobs that may need attention. The most suitable applicants seemed to be from 46-year-old Louisa Merrifield, who would act as her housekeeper and companion, and Louisa's somewhat older husband Alfred, who would act as gardener and handyman.

On 12 March 1953 the couple moved in to the bungalow on Devonshire Road, Blackpool, and Louisa Merrifield soon ingratiated herself with Sarah Ricketts – to the extent that a little over a fortnight later the old woman made a new will leaving her estate, including the bungalow, to Mrs Merrifield. When Alfred Merrifield objected to being left out, Mrs Ricketts revised it, splitting her inheritance between both the housekeeper and her husband.

Within days, thrice-married Louisa Merrifield began boasting to friends in the town that she had 'come into money.' On 25 March, while out shopping, she bumped into a former landlady and told her she had been left a bungalow worth several thousand pounds, and she was thinking of selling it and investing the money in a nursing home. This boasting and loose talk of her inheritance continued into April, when she told a friend that she had to hurry home as the lady she cared for had just died. However, later during that same chat she admitted that the woman hadn't died yet, but 'she soon will be!'

On Monday 13 April, Sarah Ricketts complained to a tradesman who delivered some groceries that the Merrifields seemed to be trying to starve her and that she suspected they were stealing from her. She told him she had changed her will in their favour, but she was planning to change it back. She died the following day.

When the reports of her death appeared in the local papers, one of those people to whom Louisa Merrifield had been boasting reported her suspicions to the police. Detectives visited the house and ordered a post-mortem. When the results revealed that the cause of death was phosphorus poisoning, officers searched the premises for a likely source, thought to be a type of rat poison.

Far left: *Sarah Ricketts.*
(T.J. Leech Archive)

Left: *Blackpool poisoner
Louisa May Merrifield, the
last woman to be hanged at
Manchester.* (TNA:PRO)

Despite the failure to find a source for the poison, the boasts made by Mrs Merrifield – that she had come into money – were enough for detectives to charge her and her husband with murder.

The Merrifields stood together before Mr Justice Glyn-Jones at Manchester at the end of July. The trial last eleven days, and although there was conflicting medical evidence that suggested that cause of death may have been due to liver failure (and no trace of poison had been found in the house), it was the loose talk that formed the bulk of the prosecution's evidence. Late in the evening on the last day of the trial, the jury returned to find Mrs Merrifield guilty of murder. They were unable to reach a verdict on her husband and he was later released when the Crown issued a *nolle prosequi* – a decline to prosecute – and he returned to Blackpool to claim his inheritance.

In the days leading up to her execution there was great deal of interest in the case. One Sunday newspaper even signed an exclusive agreement with Alfred Merrifield – who continued to visit his wife in the condemned cell while recounting their life stories in the press. A few days before the execution was scheduled, Mrs Merrifield had a blazing row during a visit and refused her husband permission for further visits.

According to assistant hangman Jock Stewart she went to her death bravely. Alfred Merrifield was outside the prison on the morning of her execution and later donated items to Tussauds' waxworks in Blackpool, where an effigy of the town's most famous murderer remains to this day. Merrifield also traded on the case for the rest of his life, giving talks and appearing in grotesque sideshows in Blackpool until his death in 1962.

*Demonstrations outside the
prison on the morning of
Mrs Merrifield's execution.*
(T.J. Leech Archive)

97

THE TENANT

Stanislaw Juras, 17 December 1953

'I want to be executed today...'

Statement made by Stanislaw Juras following conviction.

Forty-two-year-old Polish textile worker Stanislaw Juras had been lodging at a house on Trinity Place, Halifax, since arriving in the Yorkshire mill town to find work. The house, run by a Polish couple named Carol and Irena Wagner, was divided into a number of bedsits and Juras rented a room on the first floor.

On Wednesday morning, 16 September 1953, a neighbour walking past the house heard a woman scream, and at lunchtime a lodger returned to Trinity Place and found a strong smell of gas. He went to investigate and found the gas tap in the cellar had seemingly been tampered with. Having reconnected the pipe the lodger sought out Irena, whom he knew was home alone as her husband had gone to visit friends a few days earlier.

Unable to locate the landlady, he knocked on Juras' door, and although there was no answer he could tell that someone was inside. An hour later, a neighbour saw Juras climb out of his bedroom window and make off down the street: she thought this suspicious, but did nothing about it at the time.

Carol Wagner returned home that evening and was shocked to find his wife was not in their room. When he learned about the gas leak and a neighbour told him about Juras shinning down the drainpipe that afternoon, he tried the door of Juras' room; unable to force it open, he contacted the police. Inside they found the body of 29-year-old Irena Wagner lying on Juras's bed covered with a blanket. She had been strangled with a scarf and her underclothes had been removed.

Juras was arrested the following morning. When he appeared before Mr Justice Stable at Leeds Assizes in November, Juras claimed they had been having an affair and that he had killed her because she had ended their relationship. He claimed he was insane at the time and was not aware of his actions.

The prosecution claimed that there was no truth that they were having an affair and it was more likely he had lured her into his room on some pretence, possibly to do with the gas leak, before attempting to rape her. He suggested that when she resisted so strongly he had strangled her, then locked the door and fled through the window. It took the jury less than ten minutes to find him guilty as charged. Asked if he had anything to say before sentence was passed, Juras simply asked if he could be executed that day. With the black cap draped on his wig the judge told him he was unable to sanction his request, and once the sentence had been passed he was led slowly from the dock to the cells below.

Six men and one woman were convicted at Leeds Assizes that month, and as a result there was a 'death row' at the city's Armley Gaol. To ease the overcrowding, four of those sentenced were transferred to Manchester for execution. Juras was the first of them to be hanged.

98

DOUBLE LIFE

Czelslaw Kowalewski, 8 January 1954

Czelslaw Kowalewski had fallen in love. He had been courting 29-year-old Doris Allen for several months and decided he wanted to marry her. The 32-year-old Polish miner had arrived in England after the war and, after leaving a settlement camp in East Anglia, he had travelled to Leeds and found work in the coalmines. He spent his evenings drinking in public houses in the Harehills district of the city and it was here that he met Doris. They courted for six months and although they shared a flat together she only spent part of the week there, telling him she had an aged, widowed mother who needed caring for. As a result she left Kowalewski each Friday and returned on Monday.

The truth was somewhat different. Doris was not spending the weekends with her mother; neither was her mother a widow: both her parents lived across the city. Allen, it transpired, was an alias: she had a string of convictions for soliciting, and her real name was actually Doris Douglas. In fact, she was spending her weekends working as the housekeeper for 60-year-old James McGough and his 15-year-old son in a modern flat on the Quarry Bank estate.

Kowalewski was unaware of this situation until one evening in the summer of 1953: as he waited at a bus stop close to the Quarry Bank flats, he saw her leaving the building. She said she had just been to visit a friend, but when someone told him the truth about Doris' double weekend life they began a violent quarrel. She told him she was leaving and, on Friday 2 October, she said she was going to stay with her mother. When they started to quarrel she stormed out saying she wouldn't be coming back.

The following Monday evening, Doris and McGough were out drinking. McGough had arranged a darts match that night, but he left after one drink, leaving Doris at a loose end. She went across to another public house where she ran into Kowalewski. The Pole had not been to work that day and had spent the early part of the day drinking before sleeping off a hangover in a cinema. At closing time Kowalewski staggered behind her as she headed towards Quarry Bank. He said that they had sex in a doorway and he then asked her to return home with him. She refused, saying she had decided to stay with her employer.

McGough returned home later that night and neighbours heard sounds of a quarrel coming from the flat. The police were called and after ascertaining it was just a domestic they left. An hour later Kowalewski returned – but this time he burst through the door and chased Doris across the room before stabbing her several times, fatally wounding her. He fled into the night, but was arrested two days later in the Chapeltown area of the city. With Kowalewski in custody police soon built their case. There were bloodstains on his clothing and he was still in possession of the murder weapon, which detectives knew he had purchased on the day of the murder.

When he stood trial at Leeds Assizes before Mr Justice Stable in December, Kowalewski admitted he was responsible for the death of Doris Douglas, but his counsel claimed he should be guilty of manslaughter instead of murder. He stated that he had no memory of committing the crime as he was too drunk at the time to form any intention to kill.

The jury considered their verdict for just fifteen minutes before finding Kowalewski guilty of murder. Like a number of previous Leeds murders he was transferred to Manchester for execution.

Czelslaw Kowalewski. (Author's Collection)

99

TELL-TALE SLIVERS OF GLASS

James Smith, 28 November 1962

On the afternoon of Friday 4 May 1962, 57-year-old Mrs Sarah Isabella Cross was found battered to death in her little sweet and tobacconist's shop on the corner of Hulme Hall Lane and Iron Street, Miles Platting. Nine-year-old schoolgirl Stephanie Howarth had called into the shop for an ice cream and when no one came to serve her she called out. When there was no reply she stood on her tiptoes and peeped over the counter. Lying in a heap beneath the opened till was the body of the shopkeeper. Stephanie rushed home in tears shouting, 'Come quick, Auntie Belle's been killed!'

The police were called and officers at the scene found the body lying in a pool of liquid mixed with blood and with large fragments of glass scattered around. Detective Chief Superintendent Eric Cunningham led the investigation and quickly ascertained that robbery was the motive and that the kindly old lady had been murdered for the contents of the till. Her husband David told the police that the thief must have gotten away with the afternoon's takings, which would not have been a great deal of money.

Mrs Cross had been battered to death with a number of one-pint bottles; her clothing and the floor were completely soaked in lemonade. Glass fragments covered the shop floor, and the presence of five bottle tops indicated the exact number used. A sharp-eyed officer spotted a bloodstained fingerprint on a sliver of glass lying close to the door.

The shop on the corner of Iron Street and Hulme Hall Lane, where James Smith battered to death 'Belle' Cross. (Author's Collection)

It appeared that the killer was not satisfied with the contents of the till because the connecting door leading from the shop, usually kept closed, was ajar, and it looked as if he had rummaged through the desk in the sitting room. A drawer had been pulled out and its contents scattered across the carpet. The doors from the sitting room to the kitchen and from the kitchen to the backyard were open, as was the back gate leading into the street. It seemed the killer must have made his escape through the back, presumably after hearing the bell when Stephanie entered the shop.

A large number of fingerprints were found on the premises, as they would have expected given the nature of the business, but fortunately the police got a lucky break. David Cross told detectives that he had recently decorated inside the shop and other downstairs rooms, and this included painting the living-room door, which he had done just three days previously. On the edge of this door was a clear set of prints, which did not belong to either the victim or her husband. There had been no visitors since he had completed the decorating, so it was surmised that the fingerprints belonged to the killer. Cunningham had the door removed and taken to the Lancashire police headquarters at Preston, where experts combed through files for a matching print. The particles of glass were also photographed and sent to Preston.

Cunningham believed the killer was a local man, perhaps someone who passed by on his way home from work. He reasoned that the ferocity of the crime bore the hallmark of a man used to violence, and who therefore probably had a criminal record, and the chances were that his prints would be on file. While the fingerprint staff worked round the clock, Cunningham ordered a house-to-house search of all likely suspects in the area.

At the Preston headquarters a detective was given the mammoth task of reassembling the bottles. With a myriad of glass particles and a tube of glue Chief Inspector Louis Allen set about the mosaic. Some of the larger pieces matched up quite easily, and with the aid of a microscope Allen was able to piece together other fragments using the striation marks made during manufacture as a guide, each as individual as a fingerprint.

Copies of the killer's prints eventually turned up a match with prints held on file in Edinburgh. The wanted man was James Smith, a 26-year-old Scot, living with his wife and two children at 4 Corfe Street, in the Manchester suburb of Beswick. Smith worked in a factory at Failsworth and on the afternoon of the murder his route home took him past the shop.

Cunningham and Detective Inspector Tom Butcher, his second-in-command, called on Smith. He readily admitted knowing the shop where the old lady was killed. 'Everybody knows it!' he said, 'It's been on television and in the papers for the last fortnight.' He strenuously denied visiting the shop, but admitted he had walked past it on his way home from work on the day of the murder.

Cunningham ordered a thorough search of Smith's house. A vacuum cleaner was inserted down the side of the sofa and revealed a piece of glass similar to those in the reconstructed bottles. Under the microscope it was clear the glass could only have come from one of the bottles used in the attack. Satisfied that Smith was their man, he was arrested and charged with the capital murder of Mrs Isabella Cross. Detective Inspector Butcher sat with Smith moments after he had been charged. The prisoner turned to Butcher and joked, 'I'll bet you a fiver I never hang!' Not holding out much hope for the prisoner's chances, Butcher replied, 'You're on.'

Smith stood trial at Liverpool Assizes before Mr Justice Stable in October. He was charged with capital murder – in the furtherance of theft – which meant he was liable for the death penalty if found guilty. The presence of his fingerprints on the living-room door proved he had been on the shop premises, but it was the telltale sliver of glass found at his home, identical to particles from the shop and which fitted perfectly in the reconstructed bottles, that placed him there at the time of the murder.

On Wednesday morning, 28 November, James Smith was hanged. Later that morning Detectives Cunningham and Butcher visited the prison to identify the body. Looking down at the body in the mortuary, Butcher took no comfort in the fact that he had won a bet he knew he would never collect.

100

THE LAST TO HANG

Gwynne Owen Evans, 13 August 1964

In the early hours of Tuesday 7 April 1964, neighbours heard sounds of a disturbance coming from the home of 53-year-old John West on King's Avenue, Seaton, on the outskirts of Workington. Woken by a series of heavy thuds, then a scream – followed a short time later by the slamming of a car door and the screeching of tyres – neighbour Joseph Fawcett hurried to investigate. When he could get no answer he called the police. Within minutes officers arrived at the house and, after gaining entry, they found the body of John West at the foot of the stairs. He had been battered about the head and was lying, motionless and partially naked, in a pool of blood.

By 4.30 a.m., Detective Inspector John Gibson had begun the murder inquiry. There was no sign of a forced entry while a search of the house soon yielded valuable clues. On a chair in the bedroom was a neatly folded, modern-looking, off-white-coloured raincoat. It didn't look like the kind of coat a 53-year-old bachelor would wear, besides being the wrong size. One of the officers emptied the pockets.

The first item removed was a combined wallet and key holder. Inside the wallet was an army memorandum form filled out with the name Norma O'Brian and an address off Princess Road, Liverpool. Attached to the key fob were a number of Yale, locker and car keys; more importantly, there was also a medal presented by the Royal Life Saving Society in the name of 'G.O. Evans, July, 1961'.

Detectives in Liverpool found that the name on the memo form had been misspelt, and a Norma O'Brien was interviewed. She recognised the wallet and medal as belonging to Gwynne Owen Evans, a 25-year-old Londoner, whom she knew as 'Ginger', and whom she had met at Fulwood Barracks in Preston. She also gave officers an address in Cumbria where she thought Ginger lived. Officers went to the house at Camerton, three miles from Seaton, but found no one by the name Evans living there, the occupants being a family called Walby.

It took detectives a while to realise that Ginger Evans' real name was John Robson Walby and, in the meantime, a check through criminal records had given Evans' last address as Clarendon Street, Preston, ninety miles from Seaton. Officers in Preston found the house occupied by Peter Allen, who had turned twenty-one just a week earlier, and his two young sons. He confirmed that Evans, whom he knew as Sandy, rented a room in his house, and said that the lodger had gone with Mrs Allen to Manchester, where Evans was meeting his girlfriend and Mrs Allen was visiting her parents.

Allen was asked to accompany police to the station to make a statement. He gave officers an address in Manchester and Evans was picked up and questioned by officers later that afternoon.

During a search of the wanted man's belongings, an officer felt something concealed in the lining of Evans's jacket. He produced a bunch of keys, but this was not what the officer had felt so, reluctantly, Evans rummaged again in the jacket lining and withdrew a watch inscribed J.A. West. Efforts had been made to obliterate the name, but it was still clearly visible. Mrs Allen was also searched and in her basket was a blood-stained jacket which she admitted belonged to her husband. Both Evans and Allen were taken into custody and interrogated separately.

Meanwhile a post-mortem revealed that cause of death had been a fatal stab wound to the heart, but there were also thirteen split wounds to the head caused by a heavy blunt instrument, consistent with the lead pipe found beside the body. No mention of a knife had appeared in any of the newspapers reports and the general impression was that West had been battered to death.

Evans had known the dead man for several years and once worked with him briefly at the Lakeland Laundry in Workington, where West had worked for over thirty years. Evans maintained that they had remained friends and that West, who he claimed was a homosexual, had told him many times if he ever needed money, he would give him a loan.

In the spring of 1964 both Allen and Evans owed money in fines and, with Allen faced with a large rates bill, the two decided to travel to Seaton to see West about a loan. On Monday evening, 6 April, they stole a car from outside a Preston public house and, picking up Allen's wife and children who were going along for the ride, set off towards Cumbria.

According to Evans, he entered the house around 2 a.m. and West agreed to lend him money, but under certain conditions. They went up to the bedroom, where Evans took off his coat and folded it over a chair. He claimed that a short time later Allen had burst in demanding money and battered West with the heavy cosh they had taken with them, before stabbing him in the heart. At no time did Evans admit using any violence against John West. The mention of the knife was of interest to the police as no one, other than senior detectives and the pathologist, knew that a knife had been used in the murder.

Allen's account varied slightly. He said that Evans had come out of the house and beckoned him inside. Allen said he went up the stairs, whereupon West came out of the bedroom and, seeing Allen, rushed at him. Allen admitted he punched him once in the face before going into the bedroom to rummage for money and any bankbooks he could find, while Evans carried on attacking their victim on the stairs.

By the time their case came to trial at Manchester Assizes before Mr Justice Ashworth in July, the two friends had become sworn enemies following a statement Evans made, saying that he had been having an affair with Allen's wife while lodging at the Preston house.

They were charged with capital murder – during the furtherance of theft – and if convicted they faced the death penalty. The case against them was straightforward: they needed money and had gone to the house in Seaton with the intention of stealing it and, during the robbery, John West was fatally wounded. Both blamed the other for striking the fatal blow, but in the end both were deemed equally responsible and were found guilty as charged.

Allen was taken to Liverpool's Walton Gaol while Evans was taken to Strangeways Prison. They were scheduled to hang at the same moment, 8 a.m. on Thursday 13 August. At 8.30 a.m. that morning DI Gibson identified the body of Evans in the prison mortuary and was present at the inquest, which found that Gwynne Owen Evans had died as a result of judicial hanging.

Capital punishment was suspended the following year and abolished officially in 1969. They were, of course, not to know it, but the names of Allen and Evans were to pass into criminal history. They were the last to hang.

Gwynne Owen Evans, the last man to be hanged in Manchester. (Author's Collection)

Hangman Harry Allen carried out the last execution at Manchester. This photo was taken outside the prison several years into his retirement. (Author's Collection)

APPENDIX

Date of Execution	Convict	Executioner	Assistant (s)
29 March 1869	Michael James Johnson	William Calcraft	
26 December 1870	Patrick Durr	William Calcraft	
30 December 1872	Michael Kennedy	William Calcraft	William Marwood[1]
21 December 1876	William Flanagan	William Marwood	
27 March 1877	John McKenna	William Marwood	
4 February 1878	George Pigott	William Marwood	
19 November 1878	James McGowan	William Marwood	
20 May 1879	William Cooper	William Marwood	
17 February 1880	William Cassidy	William Marwood	
28 November 1881	John Aspinall Simpson	William Marwood	
13 February 1882	Richard Templeton	William Marwood	
12 February 1883	Abraham Thomas	William Marwood	
26 November 1883	Thomas Riley	Bartholomew Binns	Alfred Archer
24 November 1884+	Kay Howarth Harry Hammond Swindles	James Berry	Richard Chester
9 August 1886	Mary-Ann Britland	James Berry	
15 February 1887	Thomas Leatherbarrow	James Berry	
30 May 1887	Walter Wood	James Berry	
15 May 1888	John Alfred Gell	James Berry	
7 August 1888	John Jackson	James Berry	
24 December 1889	William Dukes	James Berry	
19 May 1891	Alfred William Turner	James Berry	
20 December 1892	Joseph Mellor	James Billington	
28 November 1893	Victor Emmanuel Hamer	James Billington	
31 July 1894	William Crossley	James Billington	
27 November 1894	James W. Whitehead	James Billington	
4 August 1896	Joseph Hurst	James Billington	
22 February 1898	George William Howe	James Billington	Thomas Billington

6 December 1899	Michael Dowdle	James Billington	William Warbrick
4 December 1900	Joseph Holden	James Billington	William Warbrick
3 December 1901	Patrick McKenna	James Billington	Henry Pierrepoint
2 December 1902	Henry McWiggins	William Billington	Henry Pierrepoint
12 May 1903	William G. Hudson	William Billington	Henry Pierrepoint
2 December 1903	Charles Wood Whittaker	John Billington	John Ellis
27 February 1906	John Griffiths	Henry Pierrepoint	John Ellis
12 May 1908	John Ramsbottom	Henry Pierrepoint	John Ellis
28 July 1908	Fred Ballington	Henry Pierrepoint	William Willis
3 August 1909	Mark Shawcross	Henry Pierrepoint	Thomas Pierrepoint
22 February 1910	Joseph Wren	Henry Pierrepoint	John Ellis
12 December 1911+	John Edward Tarkenter Walter Martyn	John Ellis	George Brown
23 July 1912	Arthur Birkett	John Ellis	Albert Lumb
13 August 1913	James Ryder	John Ellis	
17 December 1913	Ernest Edward Kelly	John Ellis	George Brown
8 March 1916	Frederick Holmes	John Ellis	Edward Taylor
29 March 1916	Reginald Haslam	John Ellis	Edward Taylor
19 December 1916	James H. Hargreaves	John Ellis	William Willis
21 March 1917	Thomas Clinton	John Ellis	
17 December 1918	William Rooney	John Ellis	
6 January 1920+	David Caplan Hyman Perdovitch	John Ellis	Robert Baxter Edward Taylor
13 April 1920	Frederick Rothwell Holt	John Ellis	William Willis
22 June 1920	William Aldred	John Ellis	William Willis
31 December 1920	Charles Colclough	John Ellis	William Willis
5 April 1921	Frederick Quarmby	John Ellis	William Willis
24 May 1921	Thomas Wilson	John Ellis	Edward Taylor
30 May 1922	Hiram Thompson	John Ellis	William Willis
3 January 1923	George F. Edisbury	John Ellis	Robert Wilson
28 March 1923	George Perry	John Ellis	
8 April 1924	Frances Wilson Booker	William Willis	Robert Baxter
13 August 1924	John Charles Horner	William Willis	Robert Wilson
26 May 1925	Patrick Power	William Willis	Thomas Phillips
11 August 1925	James Makin	William Willis	Robert Baxter
15 December 1925	Samuel Johnson	William Willis	Thomas Phillips
16 March 1926	William Henry Thorpe	William Willis	Robert Wilson
24 June 1926	Louie Calvert	Thomas Pierrepoint	William Willis
3 January 1928	Frederick Fielding	Thomas Pierrepoint	Thomas Phillips
28 June 1928	Walter Brooks	Thomas Pierrepoint	Lionel Mann
6 December 1928	Chung Yi Miao	Thomas Pierrepoint	Henry Pollard

4 April 1929	George Henry Cartledge	Thomas Pierrepoint	Robert Wilson
16 April 1931	Francis Land	Thomas Pierrepoint	Alfred Allen
15 December 1931	Solomon Stein	Thomas Pierrepoint	Thomas Phillips
3 February 1932	George Alfred Rice	Thomas Pierrepoint	Robert Wilson
18 May 1932	Charles James Cowle	Thomas Pierrepoint	Alfred Allen
19 December 1933	William Burtoft	Thomas Pierrepoint	Stanley Cross
30 May 1935	John Harris Bridge	Thomas Pierrepoint	Thomas Phillips
12 May 1936	Buck Ruxton	Thomas Pierrepoint	Robert Wilson
4 February 1937	Max Meyer Haslam	Thomas Pierrepoint	Albert Pierrepoint
12 August 1937	Horace William Brunt	Thomas Pierrepoint	Stanley Cross
20 April 1938	Charles James Caldwell	Thomas Pierrepoint	Albert Pierrepoint
11 February 1941	Clifford Holmes	Thomas Pierrepoint	Harry B. Allen
4 September 1941	John Smith	Thomas Pierrepoint	Harry B. Allen
26 July 1944	James Galbraith	Thomas Pierrepoint	Harry Kirk
9 April 1946	Harold Berry	Thomas Pierrepoint	Henry Critchell
24 April 1946	Martin Patrick Coffey	Thomas Pierrepoint	Alex Riley
27 February 1947	Walter Graham Rowland	Albert Pierrepoint	Henry Critchell
12 January 1949	Margaret Allen	Albert Pierrepoint	Harry Kirk
28 November 1950	James Henry Corbitt	Albert Pierrepoint	Herbert Allen
19 December 1950	Nicholas P. Crosby	Albert Pierrepoint	Sydney Dernley Harry Smith* Robert L. Stewart*
26 January 1951	Nenad Kovasevic	Albert Pierrepoint	Herbert Allen
8 May 1951	James Inglis	Albert Pierrepoint	Sydney Dernley
12 June 1951	John Dand	Albert Pierrepoint	Harry B. Allen
3 July 1951	Jack Wright	Albert Pierrepoint	Harry Smith
15 January 1952	Alfred Bradley	Albert Pierrepoint	Robert L. Stewart
26 February 1952	Herbert Roy Harris	Albert Pierrepoint	Robert L. Stewart
18 September 1953	Louisa May Merrifield	Albert Pierrepoint	Robert L. Stewart
17 December 1953	Stanislaw Juras	Albert Pierrepoint	Royston L. Rickard
8 January 1954	Czelslaw Kowalewski	Albert Pierrepoint	John Broadbent
28 November 1962	James Smith	Harry B. Allen	John E. Underhill
13 August 1964	Gwynne Owen Evans	Harry B. Allen	Royston L. Rickard

[1] signifies that Marwood used the alias 'John Smith' during 1872

+ signify a double execution of prisoners not connected and hanged together for separate crimes

* signify Smith and Stewart were present to witness the execution as part of their training

INDEX